MERIDIANS
Sources in World History

History 104-D

Purdue University

Pearson Learning Solutions

New York   Boston   San Francisco

London   Toronto   Sydney   Tokyo   Singapore   Madrid

Mexico City   Munich   Paris   Cape Town   Hong Kong   Montreal

Senior Vice President, Editorial and Marketing: Patrick F. Boles
Senior Sponsoring Editor: Natalie Danner
Development Editor: Mary Kate Paris
Assistant Editor: Jill Johnson
Operations Manager: Eric M. Kenney
Production Manager: Jennifer Berry
Rights Manager: Jillian Santos
Art Director and Cover Designer: Renée Sartell

Cover Art: Map of the Arctic, courtesy of the Stapleton Collection/CORBIS; map of Al Idrisi, courtesy of The Bodleian Library, University of Oxford.

Printed in the United States of America.

Please visit our website at *www.pearsoncustom.com.*

Attention bookstores: For permission to return any unsold stock, contact us at *pe-uscustomreturns@pearson.com.*

Pearson Learning Solutions, 501 Boylston Street, Suite 900, Boston, MA 02116
A Pearson Education Company
www.pearsoned.com

ISBN 10: 0-558-90394-0
ISBN 13: 978-0-558-90394-7

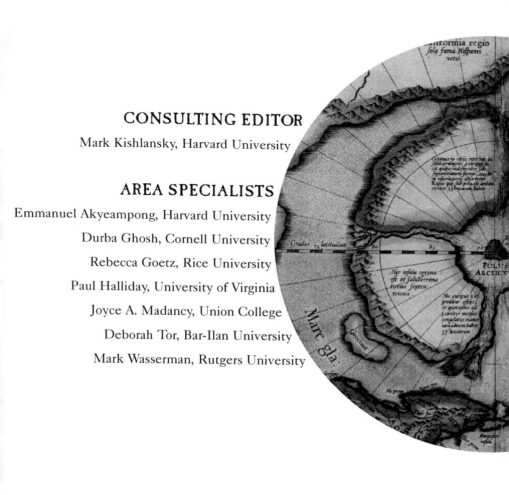

Contents

Reformation

The Unity of Classical and Christian Learning
Erasmus   1

Early Modern Exploration and Imperialism

The Evangelization of Unbelievers
Francisco de Vitoria   11

Just War
Juan Ginés de Sepúlveda   23

Scientific Revoluiton

To God Through the Stars
Jonathan Spence   31

The Slave Trade

A Venetian Describes the Portuguese West African Trade
Alvise da Cadamosto   59

Slave Trade in the Kingdom of Loango in the Eigthteenth Century
Abbé Proyart   71

from Chapter 3, "The Slaveship," in "Equiano's Travels"
Olaudah Equiano   77

Slave in a New World
Aphra Behn   87

The Views of Osei Bonsu
Joseph Dupuis 97

Nineteenth-Century Imperialism

Travels in West Africa
Mary Kingsley 103

from "Things Fall Apart"
Chinua Achebe 111

Methods of Native Administration: Political Officers and Native Rulers
Lord Frederick Lugard 117

World War I

Storm of Steel
Ernst Jünger 129

Decolonization

Continental Government for Africa
Kwame Nkrumah 135

from Congo My Country
Patrice Lumumba 143

OAU Charter
The Organization for African Unity 153

Reformation

THE UNITY OF CLASSICAL AND CHRISTIAN LEARNING

Erasmus

*Born as an illegitimate child in Rotterdam, Desiderius Erasmus (c. 1466–
1536) eventually became known as the leading humanist of his day. Although
his natural inclination toward peace and conciliation eventually put him at
odds both with the great Protestant controversialist Martin Luther as well as
with more doctrinaire Catholics, his writings had a huge influence on his contemporaries and continue to be studied today.*

*At the age of nine Erasmus entered a school in Deventer run by the
Brethren of the Common Life, where he received a sound education in the classics. After the death of his parents he joined a religious order, the Augustinian
Canons of Steyn (1487), a move that he later regretted, finding himself un-
suited to the monastic life; in 1517 he finally obtained a papal dispensation
from his vows and returned officially to lay status. By that time, indeed, he
had left the monastery far behind, having become secretary to the bishop of
Cambrai in 1493 and having received permission to study theology in Paris in
1495. The intellectual climate in Paris was nearly as distasteful to Erasmus as
that of the monastery—he cared neither for scholastic theology nor for college
food – and he left without a degree after less than four years. Erasmus's subsequent life involved a great deal of travel throughout Europe where he came
to know many of the rulers and intellectual leaders of his day. In 1499 he
traveled to England, where he made friends with Thomas More and John*

Reprinted from *The Essential Erasmus*, translated by John P. Dolan, by permission of Dutton
Signet, a division on Penguin Group (USA) Inc. Copyright © 1964 by John P. Dolan.

Colet; in 1506 he went south to Italy, coming in contact with the humanist circle of Aldus Manitius in the great printing center of Venice; in 1509 he returned to England, where he taught Greek for a time at the University of Cambridge. In 1514 he was back on the Continent, residing in Louvain, where he had relationships with the university's faculty of theology, but his application of philology to the Scriptures and reluctance to condemn Luther bred hostility against him. Erasmus then moved to Basel (1521–29) and, upon the city's becoming Protestant, to the nearby Catholic town of Freiburg im Breisgau. He was back in Basel working on the publication of one of his works when he died on July 12, 1536.

Erasmus was viewed with suspicion, during his lifetime and afterward, both by Protestants and Catholics. His longing for a return to the simplicity of the Gospel and his advocacy of an inner spiritual life, in contrast with excessive dependence on outward rituals, placed him close in spirit to Luther and his followers. At the same time, he never parted ways with the Catholic church. He differed with Luther fundamentally concerning the relationship between man and divine grace, and feared the social and political consequences of the Reformation. In particular, he feared that Europe would be torn apart by war and religious controversy and hoped that the mild voice of reason would prevail over polemics. Erasmus was viewed as the ideal type of the Christian humanist, one who combined great learning in the classics with sincere piety. Erasmus was a superb stylist and promoter of the classics and the ancient Church Fathers, and was among the first scholars to apply humanist philological methods to the study of the Bible. His critical edition of the New Testament, which included the Greek text and Erasmus's revised translation of the Latin Vulgate, appeared in 1516 and is considered one of his most significant accomplishments.

One of the early works that established Erasmus's reputation throughout Europe was the Handbook of the Militant Christian (or Enchiridion Militis Christiani), which appeared in Latin in 1503 and was soon translated into many languages. The work originated in a pious woman's concern for the spiritual state of her wayward husband, but Erasmus provided much more than a call to repentance. The booklet is a handbook of spiritual devotion, which first encourages the reader to practice an inward piety, and then provides a set of practical rules for resisting temptation and sin. The present selection, taken from the first section, illustrates Erasmus's Christian humanism and his twin

2

emphasis on prayer and knowledge. For Erasmus, learning encompasses knowledge both of the Scriptures and of the classics; the two forms of knowledge are inseparable and mutually reinforcing. To make this case, Erasmus favors an allegorical form of interpretation that finds Christian lessons in the pagan classics as well as humanistic lessons in the Bible. His emphasis on this style of interpretation and on the writings of the Church Fathers was related to his distaste for scholastic theology and interest in a personal and practical piety that prepares one for spiritual warfare.

I think we can truthfully say that nothing is more important in military training than a thorough knowledge of the weapons to be employed and the nature of the enemy to be encountered. I would add to this that the need for preparedness, of having the weapons close at hand, is also of the utmost importance. In ordinary warfare it is customary that leave of absence or actual retirement to winter quarters brings about a cessation of hostilities from time to time. This is certainly not the case in the kind of warfare we are describing. We can never permit ourselves to be even a finger's length from our weapons. Since our enemy is incessant in his attacks, we must be constantly on the battle line, constantly in a state of preparedness. As a matter of fact, our enemy, when he appears peaceful, when he feigns flight or a truce, can at that very moment be assumed to be preparing for an attack. He is most dangerous when he appears peaceful, and it is during his violent attacks that we can actually feel most secure. It is for this reason that our primary concern must be to keep the mind armed. Our enemies are armed for no other purpose than to destroy us; surely we should not be ashamed to take up arms so as not to perish.

We will speak about Christian armor more in detail when we treat that subject later on. Meanwhile I would like to point out briefly two weapons that we should prepare to use in combating the chief vices. These weapons are prayer and knowledge. St. Paul clearly expresses the desire that men be continually armed when he commands us to pray without ceasing. Pure prayer directed to heaven is able to subdue passion, for it is, as it were, a citadel inaccessible to the enemy. Knowledge, or learning, fortifies the mind with salutary precepts and keeps virtue ever before us. These two are inseparable, the former imploring but the latter suggesting what should be

3

prayed for. St. James tells us that we should pray always for faith and hope, seeking the things of salvation in Jesus' name. We may recall that Christ asked the sons of Zebedee if they really knew what they were praying for. We must always emphasize the dual necessity of both prayer and knowledge. In your flight from sin imitate Aaron as a model of prayer and Moses as an example of knowledge of the law. Neither allow your knowledge to lessen nor your prayer to become sterile.

Listen for a moment to what Christ has to say in Matthew's Gospel: "But in praying, do not multiply words, as the Gentiles do; for they think that by saying a great deal, they will be heard. So do not be like them; for your Father knows what you need before you ask Him." And St. Paul condemns ten thousand words spoken with the lips in favor of five uttered in understanding. Moses spoke nothing yet he heard the words, "Why do you call after me?" It is not the loud sound of the mouth, but rather the pleas of an ardent soul that reach the divine ear. Try to let this be a practice with you: When the enemy assaults you and the other vices give you trouble, lift up your mind to heaven and in your faith do not fail to raise up your hands also. Perhaps the best remedy in this matter is to be continually occupied with works of piety so that you will revert, not to worldly affairs, but to Christ.

You must believe me when I say that there is really no attack from the enemy, no temptation so violent, that a sincere resort to Holy Writ will not easily get rid of it. There is no misfortune so sad that a reading of the Scriptures does not render bearable. Therefore, if you will but dedicate yourself entirely to the study of the Scriptures, if you meditate day and night on the divine law, nothing will ever terrorize you and you will be prepared against any attack of the enemy.

I might also add that a sensible reading of the pagan poets and philosophers is a good preparation for the Christian life. We have the example of St. Basil, who recommends the ancient poets for their natural goodness. Both St. Augustine and St. Jerome followed this method. St. Cyprian has worked wonders in adorning the Scriptures with the literary beauty of the ancients. Of course it is not my intention that you imbibe the bad morals of the pagans along with their literary excellence. I am sure that you will nonetheless find many examples in the classics that are conducive to right living. Many of these writers were, of course, very good teachers of ethics.

4

We have the example of Moses, who did not spurn the advice of Jethro. These readings mature us and constitute a wonderful preparation for an understanding of the Scriptures. I feel this is quite important, because to break in upon these sacred writings without this preparation is almost sacrilegious. St. Jerome assails the presumption of those who, even though they may be learned in other fields, presume to expatiate on the Bible. You can imagine the audacity of those who, having no preparation whatsoever, try to do the same thing.

We must not persist in clinging to the letter, and the reading of Homer and Virgil will be of no use unless we look to its allegorical side. If you like the classics, then you will understand what I mean. If the obscene passages in the ancients bother you, then by all means refrain from reading them. Of all the philosophical writings I would recommend the Platonists most highly. For not only their ideas but their very mode of expression approaches that of the Gospels. Of course they should be read in a cursory manner, and whatever is of real value in them should be applied and referred to Christ. If to the pure of heart all things are clean, then to the impure everything appears to be unclean. Whenever the reading of secular selections arouses your baser appetites, then leave them alone.

Reading the Scriptures with a clean heart is a basic rule. It prevents what is intended to be medicinal from becoming noxious. You must maintain at all times a high regard for the revealed word. It is genuine because it has its origin in the very mind of God. If you approach the Scriptures in all humility and with regulated caution, you will perceive that you have been breathed upon by the Holy Will. It will bring about a transformation that is impossible to describe. You will perceive the delights of the Blessed Bridegroom; you will see the riches of Solomon. The hidden treasures of eternal wisdom will be yours. Yet I would caution you. The entrance to this abode of wisdom is narrow. The doorway is low, and there is danger in not stooping when you enter. There is nothing that you can believe with greater certitude than what you read in these writings. The senses themselves cannot offer greater certainty. Divine revelation has made it clear that heaven and earth will not pass away before all that is contained therein is fulfilled. Man may lie and make mistakes; the truth of God neither deceives nor is deceived.

5

Let me mention another requirement for a better understanding of Holy Scripture. I would suggest that you read those commentators who do not stick so closely to the literal sense. The ones I would recommend most highly after St. Paul himself are Origen, Ambrose, Jerome, and Augustine. Too many of our modern theologians are prone to a literal interpretation, which they subtly misconstrue. They do not delve into the mysteries, and they act as if St. Paul were not speaking the truth when he says that our law is spiritual. There are some of these theologians who are so completely taken up with these human commentators that they relegate what the Fathers had to say to the realm of dreams. They are so entranced with the writings of Duns Scotus that, without ever having read the Scriptures, they believe themselves to be competent theologians. I care not how subtle their distinctions are; they are certainly not the final word on what pertains to the Holy Spirit.

If your interest in sacred doctrine revolves more about what is vital and dynamic rather than merely dialectical, if you incline more toward what moves the inner man than to what leads to empty arguments, then read the Fathers. Their deep piety has withstood the test of time. Their very thoughts constitute a prayerful meditation, and they penetrate into the very depths of the mysteries they propound. I do not mean to condemn modern theologians; I am merely pointing out that in view of our purpose, namely, a more practical piety, they are hardly to be recommended. Let us not forget that the Divine Spirit has its own manner of speaking and its own figures of speech. Learn these from the very outset. The Divine Wisdom speaks to us and, like an attentive mother, adjusts Her language to our infancy. For the tiny infants She provides milk and for the sick, herbs. To receive solid food you must grow up spiritually. She lowers Herself to your humility. You must raise yourself to Her sublimity. To remain like an infant is unfortunate. Unending illness is reprehensible. Pluck the marrow from the broken bone: meditation upon a single verse gives more nourishment, brings more wisdom, than continued verbal repetition of the whole psalm.

I warn you with the more diligence because I know that this error has confused, not merely the crowd, but also those who in name and in garb claim perfect religion. These people believe the greatest piety is repeating as many psalms as possible every day, though they scarcely understand

6

them. On every side monastic piety grows cold, languishes, and disappears because the monks grow old and gray in the letter of the Scriptures rather than maturing to a spiritual understanding. They fail to hear Christ proclaiming in the Gospel, "The flesh profits nothing, it is the spirit that gives life." We know the law is spiritual. Spiritual things should not be made carnal. In times past the Father was worshipped in the mountains. Now He wants to be worshipped in the spirit.

I do not want to be misunderstood. I by no means despise the weakness of those who, from feebleness of mind, do the only things they are able to do. Certain words in magic rituals are thought efficacious even when those who pronounce them do so without understanding them. Likewise, divine words, though little understood, should be believed beneficial for those who speak or hear them in sincere faith and pure affection. The angels who are present bring assistance. Nor, indeed, does Paul condemn those who sing in the spirit or those who speak in tongues. But he does urge a fuller use of graces. Of course there is no shame for those prevented from better things by vice, not of the mind, but of nature. As St. Paul has said, "Let not him who eats despise him who does not eat; and let not him who does not eat judge him who eats."

However, I do not want you who are better endowed to remain content with the barren letter. Rather, I want you to pass on to the more profound mysteries. Strengthen yourselves with frequent prayer, until He who holds the key of David, who closes and no one opens, will open for you the book sealed with the seven seals—the secrets of the Father, which no one knows except the Son and he to whom the Son deigns to reveal them.

But how should you pray? I intended to describe a way of life, not a method of learning. Yet I deviated a bit to point out an arsenal of weapons that you could profitably use in this new type of warfare. So pick out from pagan books whatever is best. In studying the ancients follow the example of the bee flying about the garden. Like the bee, suck out only what is wholesome and sweet; reject what is useless and poisonous. Follow this rule, and your mind will be better clothed. Then you will enter into the battle of daily life better armed. Nonetheless, whenever you find truth and virtue, refer it to Christ. If you wish to consult the treasure house of Paul, that valiant captain, there you will discover "that the weapons of our warfare are not of the flesh, but are mighty before God for the destruction of

7

fortifications, destroying counsels and every height that tends to bar the knowledge of God." You will find the weapons of God by which you can endure an evil day. On your right you will find the arms of justice, on your left the armor of truth, the breastplate of justice, and the shield of faith, a shield with which you can ward off the fiery darts of the devil. You will find also the helmet of salvation and the sword of the spirit, which is the word of God. Carefully fortified with these weapons, a man can fearlessly utter those courageous words of Paul: "Who shall separate us from the love of Christ? Shall tribulation, or distress, or famine, or peril, or persecution, or the sword?" See the many enemies the devil directs and how frightened they are at everything. But hear something stronger. Paul adds, "But in all these things we conquer because of Him who has loved us. For I am sure that neither death, nor life, nor angels, nor principalities, nor powers, nor things present, nor any other creatures shall be able to separate us from the love of God which is in Christ Jesus." What a happy confidence the arms of light give to Paul, an insignificant man who called himself a castoff of the world!

But to return to our original purpose. We must forge a handy weapon, an *enchiridion,* a dagger, that you can always carry with you. You must be on guard when you eat or sleep, even when you travel in the course of worldly concerns and perhaps become weary of bearing this righteous armor. Never allow yourself to be totally disarmed, even for a moment, lest your wily foe oppress you. Do not be ashamed to carry this little sword with you. For it is neither a hardship to bear nor useless in defending yourself. Though it is a small weapon, it will enable you, if you use it skillfully, to withstand the enemy's tumultuous assaults quite easily and avoid a deadly wound. Now is the time for us to teach ourselves a kind of "manual of arms." I promise that, if you diligently train yourself in it, our sovereign Lord, Jesus Christ, will transfer you, rejoicing and victorious, from this garrison to the city of Jerusalem, where there is neither tumult nor war at all, but everlasting peace and perfect tranquillity. Meanwhile all hope of safety should be placed in your arms and your armor.

QUESTIONS

1. What ideas about Christianity does Erasmus promote by use of the metaphor of warfare? What are the Christian's weapons? Who or what is the enemy?

2. How does Erasmus use the Bible to explain his ideas about prayer? How should the Bible be read?

3. Why should a Christian read the "pagan poets" as well as the Bible?

4. Why does Erasmus dislike the work of "modern" theologians?

Early Modern Exploration and Imperialism

DOCUMENT

THE EVANGELIZATION
OF UNBELIEVERS

Francisco de Vitoria

In Spain and its colonies during the sixteenth century there was a lively debate over whether or not Spain had acted morally in acquiring its empire in the Americas. At the heart of the controversy were two issues. First, were the Spaniards justified in conquering the indigenous peoples in order to convert them to Christianity and, second, were the Spaniards justified in conquering the indigenous in order to carry on free trade?

Francisco de Vitoria (1485–1536), a Dominican friar, was one of the leading theologians of his time. From his professorship at the University of Salamanca, Vitoria rejected the contemporary justifications for Spanish rule in the Americas. He denied that the indigenous peoples were inferior to the Spaniards. He did not believe the Spanish were entitled to their empire through the right of discovery, nor because the lands were vacant. Vitoria instead maintained that the Spaniards were entitled to free passage through the Americas. Because the Indians violated the Spaniards' right to communication and travel, the latter could legitimately wage war to assure these rights. The Spaniards, he also asserted, had the right to preach the gospel, stop cannibalism, and eliminate tyrannical rulers. He justified the Spanish conquest in these terms.

In this selection, Vitoria takes on the explosive question as to whether or not the Spanish had the right to force the Indians to adopt Christianity.

Reprinted from *Political Writings,* by permission of Cambridge University Press. Copyright © 1991 by Anthony Pagden.

11

SHOULD UNBELIEVERS BE FORCIBLY CONVERTED?

§1 Aquinas replies by establishing a preliminary distinction, namely, that the unbelievers in question are *those who have never taken the faith.* These *should not be forcibly converted;* but a second conclusion is that they may be *forcibly restrained from hindering the missionaries of the faith,* and from insulting Christ and Christians; this is clear, because everyone has the right to defend himself and his temporal interests, and therefore also his spiritual interests. And his third conclusion is that those who have received the faith may be forced back to the faith; see the explicit testimonies he adduces. . . .

A DOUBT ARISES by what law it is prohibited to forcibly convert unbelievers? To harm another is prohibited by natural law; but to force these people to believe is not to harm them, but to help them; *ergo.* The reply is that it is prohibited in many passages of human law; therefore this is no objection, because positive law cannot forbid anything unless it is prohibited in divine law. I conclude that it is prohibited in divine law.

A doubt then arises as to where this prohibition is to be found? Not in Scripture, because if it was there Saint Thomas would have cited it among his authorities, being always a most careful researcher in this respect. I reply that there are no unequivocal authorities to this effect, but that there are some passages from which it may be inferred, though not clearly, at least by deduction. This is as much to say, it comes not from positive divine law but from natural law; and the arguments for proving it depend on natural reason. . . . Thomist theologians also advance the following proof for the conclusion: Evil means are not justified even by good ends. But to apply coercion to anyone is evil; therefore, unbelievers cannot lawfully be compelled to believe. This argument, however, perhaps involves a *petitio principii.*

ON THIS BASIS, one could construct an *a posteriori* proof of Saint Thomas's conclusion: namely, that *more harm than good follows from forcible conversion, which is therefore unlawful:*

1. In the first place, forcible conversion would cause great provocation and unrest (*scandulum*) among the heathen. . . .

2. The second bad effect is that, instead of the benevolent and proper affection required for belief, forcible conversion would generate immense hate in them, and that in turn would give rise to pretense and hypocrisy.

12

We could never be sure whether or not they truly believed in their hearts; there would be nothing to move them to have faith, only intimidation and threats. Their conversion would be empty and ineffective. Again, as Richard of Middleton says, no one can believe unless he wills; but the will cannot be compelled, *ergo*. Besides, license to compel men in this way would be harmful, because if anyone could forcibly convert men to their own religion, the more powerful would drag many more into following their own evil heresies.

§2 NEVERTHELESS, Duns Scotus, in the passage cited above, holds that the opposing argument is, if not true, at least more probable; that is, that *if precautions are taken to ensure that these evil and undesirable consequences are avoided, a prince may forcibly convert pagans who live in his own kingdom:*

1. (. . .)

2. Consequently, assuming for the sake of argument that such an enactment is properly promulgated and published, all are obliged to believe in Christ, and they commit a sin if they refuse to accept the Christian religion.

3. The prince is empowered to punish and coerce those who commit this sin, just as he is for any other sin; further, by thus coercing them, the prince does not harm them, but benefits them; therefore he can coerce them.

4. "Ignorance makes an act involuntary," as is clear from Aristotle's *Nicomachean Ethics* 1110b 17–24; hence there is no injury (*iniuria*) to our Saracen because he *would* accept Christianity if he knew it was better, but in fact he is ignorant of the faith. Hence his conversion is not involuntary; formally it may be so, but effectively it is voluntary. In the same way, in giving medicine to a patient who does not know that it is good for him, the doctor does no injury (*iniuria*) to the sick man; the latter takes the medicine without formally wishing to do so, to be sure, but in effect he does so willingly.

5. Again, if someone wished to commit suicide, I should be obliged to prevent him from doing so if I could by confiscating his weapons; I am therefore all the more obliged to prevent him from committing spiritual suicide.

6. Furthermore, the commonwealth has the authority to enact laws not

only in civil matters, but also in matters of religion; this is part of natural law. Hence every Christian commonwealth has this power to use forcible conversion; *ergo*, any Christian king or commonwealth may lawfully compel their subjects to accept the Christian faith.

7. Their own priests have the power by natural law to instruct them and enact laws in religious matters, and their subjects are bound to obey them under pain of mortal sin, if the law is good. Hence a Christian prince may also compel his own subjects to accept his faith.

BUT ON THE OTHER HAND we must reply to this question by going back to our distinction. Some unbelievers are subjects of Christian princes, such as the Saracens who have settled in Spain; but *others are not subjects.*

I REPLY by asserting, first, that to compel those who are subjects is not intrinsically evil, like perjuring an oath; that is, it is not so evil that it cannot sometimes be a good deed. "It is evil," as Saint Thomas says, "but not so evil that it can never be good"; the proof being that it is not by definition so evil as to involve an inevitable breach of charity toward God or one's neighbor. It is not contrary to God's interest; indeed, it is clearly a great advancement of the Christian religion. Nor is it against our neighbor's interest, since it is to his benefit. The confirmation is that when we say something is "lawful," we are not obliged to prove the assertion until contrary proof is offered that it is harmful, according to the decretals *Sicut noxius* (X.2.23.1, and X.1.12.1). In the question under consideration, forcible conversion is in itself lawful, or at least not unlawful, and I am therefore not bound to prove that it is lawful.

Second, I assert that Christian princes have the authority to compel their subjects to believe; that is, if it be lawful to compel unbelievers. Christian princes may compel their own subjects not only in civil matters but also in religious ones; the commonwealth holds both civil and religious authority over its own subjects by natural law, and the prince has the same authority as the commonwealth over his subjects, be they pagans or not. Therefore, that the prince may not so compel them must be due not to lack of power, but to the expediency or otherwise of the policy.

Third, I agree with Saint Thomas that forcible conversion is evil. This is clear from the proof of the reply to the second argument, in the canon *De Iudaeis* (*Decretum* D.45.5).

Fourth, I assert that even if it is not evil *per se,* it is evil because of the evil consequences which it entrains. The proof that it is evil *per se* is that if faith must be received voluntarily, no one can receive it by coercion. And the undesirable consequences mentioned above need no further comment. They are confirmed by experience; we see that Saracens never become Christians; no, indeed, they are as much Moors as ever they were (*tan moros son agora como antes*).

Fifth, if all the evils and undesirable consequences are tolerable, Scotus's opinion is tenable. And this is what Scotus means when he says "if precautions are taken to ensure that evil and undesirable consequences are avoided." To do so, however, is difficult. Nevertheless, if the consequences can be avoided, it will be lawful to use forcible conversion, as Scotus says. The confirmation is to be found in Saint Thomas, *Summa Theologica* I-II.92.1, where he enquires what is the purpose of civil, that is, royal, power and replies that it is not only to preserve peace and good neighborliness, but also to make the citizens good and happy. But no one can be good unless he is Christian and accepts our faith; *ergo.* This is further confirmed by the fact that, from the standpoint of natural law, a prince or commonwealth is empowered to use coercion on them; hence a Christian prince to whom they are subject (may use coercion to convert them). . . .

TO THE FIRST, concerning Duns Scotus's argument concerning King Sisebut, I reply that the king is praised for his zeal and piety, but not for the deed itself, which indeed earned him a rebuke for breaking the strict prohibition against any forcible baptism of unbelievers. And the text of the canon also adduces the argument that God "hath mercy on whom He will have mercy, and whom He will he hardeneth" (Romans 9:18), for faith is a gift from God. All the same, Sisebut was a most pious king, and was perhaps counselled by his bishops to use force in that way.

TO THE SECOND, even granting that they are obliged to receive the faith, this argument implies only that forcible baptism is lawful, and hence that if there are no undesirable consequences they may be coerced. But this does not contradict Saint Thomas.

15

TO THE THIRD we may reply in the same way. In addition, I assert that an injustice (*iniuria*) is done them, because their liberty is taken away. If a king were to force someone to take a rich and beautiful woman to wife, even a princess, although he might be obliged to marry her and might even find it hard to make a better match, he would nevertheless be wronged if he was coerced.

TO THE FOURTH, that those who are unwilling through ignorance are not in effect being coerced at all, the reply is that this argument proves only that forcible baptism would be lawful if there were no undesirable consequences; but that is all. In addition, I assert that a wrong is done to them, and that they are indeed acting under compulsion "formally speaking"—just like the man who is compelled to marry a wife who is good, but of whom he himself is invincibly ignorant.

TO THE FIFTH I reply that it remains dangerous to coerce anyone in matters of religion, however advisable it may be in other cases. Therefore the analogy is valid.

. . .

THIS CONCLUDES WHAT I HAVE TO SAY about unbelievers who are subjects.

⊕

§3 IT MAY BE ASKED, however, regarding the other kind who are not subjects, *whether Christian princes can convert them by violence and the sword, if no scandal or undesirable consequences ensue?* The reply is that they cannot, because the king of Spain has no greater power over them than I do over my fellow citizens; but I cannot compel a fellow citizen to hear Mass; *ergo.*

A DOUBT ARISES whether, given that these unbelievers cannot be compelled to keep the Christian law in this way, *whether they can be compelled to keep the law of nature, which is common to all?* Some reply that they can; that our king can compel these barbarians to keep the law of nature just as I can compel someone not to commit suicide. They prove this by saying that all men profess the law of nature; and, as Saint Thomas puts it, "Whoever accepts the law of Christ can be compelled to keep it."

The reply to this is that there are some sins against nature which are harmful to our neighbors, such as cannibalism or euthanasia of the old and senile, which is practiced in Terra Firma [evidently the American mainlands]; and since the defense of our neighbors is the rightful concern of each of us, even for private persons and even if it involves shedding blood, it is beyond doubt that any Christian prince can compel them not to do these things. By this title alone the emperor is empowered to coerce the Caribbean Indians (*insulani*).

Second, I assert that princes can compel unbelievers who are their temporal subjects to abandon their sins against the commonwealth, because they are subject in temporal matters to their kings. And since the emperor is empowered to make laws for the utility of the commonwealth, if there are any sins against the temporal and human good of the commonwealth, he can compel them to abandon them.

Third, I assert that the faithful cannot compel unbelievers to keep an obvious law of nature, unless it is necessary for the good and peace of the Christian commonwealth, or unless its breach harms a neighbor in the way I have explained. This I think is most certain. Nor do they have any right to act against the infidels solely on the grounds that the latter do not observe the law of nature. If they did have such a right, a Christian king could also compel them to abandon their idols, and that would mean leaving them without any law. That is false; *ergo*.

A DOUBT ARISES whether it is lawful to smash down the idols of these barbarians, once the faith has been preached to them and they have refused to accept it? It seems that it is lawful because it does them no harm or wrong. The reply is that it is not evil *per se* to do so, being against neither the honor of God nor the good of a neighbor, since it does not harm them. But I say that this ought not to be done on every occasion, primarily because it may provoke their fierce indignation, and destroy any kind feelings toward us which they may happen to have. Among peoples where the majority have been converted, however, or where it is to be hoped they may be converted by such actions, it will be quite lawful. I say the same of their temples; they should not be thrown down, because this is an injury (*iniuria*) to their rights, and because even after they are thrown down, they will rebuild them.

§4 A FURTHER DOUBT ARISES *whether unbelievers may at least be indirectly coerced,* for instance, by taxes and levies by which they may be encouraged to become converts to the faith? . . .

IN THIS REGARD, it should be noted that "taxes (*tributum*) and levies (*exactio*)" are of two kinds. One kind may justly be imposed on unbelievers even without their being converted to the faith, such as tributes appropriate to the time and place raised at the outbreak of war, which even unbelievers can understand to be just; the proof is that such tributes could be imposed on them even if they were Christians, and may therefore be imposed on them while they are still unbelievers (I am talking, of course, of unbelievers who live in Christian lands and are subjects of Christian princes). Indeed, they may be required to pay tributes from which Christians are exempted, so long as their fiscal burden is moderate and not increased by the fact that Christians are exempted.

Second, I assert that if the tribute is unjust and immoderate, it cannot be demanded of them. From this it follows that the king can justly order the expulsion of the Saracens from our country if they pose a probable threat of subverting the faithful or overturning the homeland. He may legitimately do this because, even if he knows that it may cause them to be converted to the faith, they are not thereby forced to convert. He could not do it, perhaps with the actual intention of using the fear of exile, which affects even the most strong-minded of men, to effect their conversion; but, as long as that intention is absent, he is empowered to use his rights, whatever the consequences. If he cannot exercise direct compulsion over them, he can make a law ordering the exile from his kingdom of anyone who refuses to become a Christian. That this is lawful is proved by the fact that in other matters where compulsion is unlawful, he may employ the same device. For instance, the law states that any Saracen who sleeps with a Christian woman is punishable by death. If one were caught doing so, the king is empowered to put him to death, whether he sticks to his perfidious creed or whether he becomes a Christian; but he also has the power to pardon him from the death penalty if he is willing to become a Christian, even though his conversion would have come about under fear of death. This would be perfectly fair, because the king would be using his rights.

But as for tributes which cannot also be demanded of the faithful, I assert that they cannot be demanded of unbelievers with the intention of making them convert. Unbelievers cannot be deprived of their goods on the grounds of their unbelief, any more than other Christians, because they possess true right of ownership (*dominium rerum*) over their own property.

By the same token, it is clear that they cannot be burdened with greater fiscal obligations than are lawful in the case of the faithful. . . .

For that purpose, yes; but could they impose heavier taxes on them to force them to convert? This is still in doubt, since we agree that it is not lawful to use fear and violence to convert them. For myself, I have little doubt that more of them could be converted by greater leniency; and they would be likely to remain firmer in the faith. See Saint Thomas's *Opusculum XXI ad ducissam Brabantiae,* where he explains all this: how the prince may impose heavier taxes on them than on Christians, but not excessive ones, and many other useful remarks on the subject.

§5 IT IS ARGUED, nevertheless, that they can be directly compelled, because Saint Thomas says that they can be compelled *for blasphemy.* But all unbelievers blaspheme continually; therefore it is always lawful to compel them, because they hinder our faith with their blasphemies.

The reply is that unbelievers may blaspheme in two ways. The first is if their blasphemies are an injury (*iniuria*) or impediment to Christians, for instance, if they were to send us a letter full of blasphemies. In this case we may set aside any question of faith; we may go to war against them solely on the grounds that they have done us injury (*iniuria*). But if they keep their blasphemies to themselves, we cannot use this alone as grounds for declaring war against them. We are well aware that both Jews and heathens blaspheme the name of Christ among themselves, but we cannot for this reason alone go to war with them.

A DOUBT ARISES whether princes may lawfully coerce them with threats and intimidation? It seems that they can, because Christ forced Paul to believe by casting him to the ground and blinding him (Acts 9:3–9); therefore the same can be done to unbelievers. The reply is that it is not lawful for all of us to do everything which God is permitted to do, because we are not the masters of mankind as Christ is. Hence, Christ could coerce not only Paul, but the whole world, and He could have left this power to the Church; but He did not. Second, I reply that if it were in our power to move hearts, as Christ could, then it would be lawful for us to behave in this way; but He made Paul believe, not by intimidation but by divine inspiration. It is clear from this that masters, contrary to their own belief, do not have the power to put their infidel servants to death, nor to inflict unjust punishments on them. It is lawful, on the other hand, to give preferential treatment to those of their slaves who are Christians, as opposed to those who are not, as Nicolaus de Tudeschis [1386–1445, canon lawyer and archbishop of Palermo] says of the Jews in his commentary on the decretal *Nouit* (X.2.1.13), where he also holds that unbelievers can be compelled to observe the whole of natural law, because they can be restrained from committing homicide, and also from usury, as stated in the decretal *Usurarum* (*Sext* 5.5.1). But it will not always be lawful to compel them in every matter to do with natural law; they cannot be forcibly compelled to abandon polygamy, for example, or other such practices. In fact, Nicolaus de Tudeschis's examples only serve to prove what I have already said, namely, that they can be forced not to upset the commonwealth, and not to harm their Christian neighbors.

A FINAL DOUBT ARISES whether unbelievers who have not themselves received the faith, but whose parents were converts who have since apostatized, can be forcibly baptized? In other words, can someone who is not baptized but whose father was baptized be compelled to accept baptism? The question is raised by Pierre de la Palu [ca. 1270/1280–1342, a Dominican and titular patriarch of Jerusalem] in his commentary on Lombard's *Sentences* IV.4.4. He comes to no firm decision, but seems to be saying that they can be compelled because the Church has the right to enforce baptism on the children of Christians even against their own or their parents' will, and there is no apparent reason why it should have lost this right in the present case; therefore the Church can use compulsion. I believe that in this case they should indeed be compelled. But against this, it would follow that the Christians can compel Saracens any of whose forefathers were baptized. For example, let us suppose for the argument that the present-day Saracens are separated from these forefathers by ten generations; the argument then runs that the Church had the right to baptize the children of their forefather nine generations back, and hence the children of their forefather eight generations back, and so on down to the present generation; *ergo*. In reply, one may say that if it could be established beyond doubt that these Saracens were the distant descendants of Christians, and if they could be forcibly converted without provocation, then it ought to be done. But the Church does not do so, because it cannot be established, and also because of the inevitable unrest which would ensue.

QUESTIONS

1. According to Vitoria, how should the Spaniards treat unbelievers?
2. What is the most compelling reason Vitoria presents for not coercing conversion to Christianity?
3. In what ways can kings treat non-Christians differently than Christians?
4. Do you think that the philosophical/ethical debates at Salamanca had real effect in the empire on a daily basis?

JUST WAR

Juan Ginés de Sepúlveda

In Spain and its colonies during the sixteenth century there was a lively debate over whether or not Spain had acted morally in acquiring its empire in the Americas. At the heart of the controversy were two issues. First, were the Spaniards justified in conquering the indigenous peoples in order to convert them to Christianity and, second, were the Spaniards justified in conquering the indigenous in order to carry on free trade? The arguments bore in on the very nature of the indigenous peoples. To those who believed that the Spaniards rightfully conquered the Americas and subjugated its peoples, the Indians were incontrovertibly inferior. They maintained that the Indians were cruel barbarians, who worshiped idols and acted promiscuously.

Juan Ginés de Sepúlveda (1490–1573) was a Spanish scholar who was a well-known opponent of Bartolomé de las Casas. De Las Casas had conducted a campaign against the mistreatment of the indigenous peoples in the new Spanish empire in the Americas. Sepúlveda, in contrast, defended the right of the Spanish to conquer the indigenous peoples, maintaining that the superior Spaniards were actually acting charitably in bringing civilization and Christianity to the natives.

In this selection Sepúlveda argues that the Spanish could offer "barbarians" the opportunity to obtain the benefits of civilization, most importantly Christianity, under the auspices of the King of Spain. If they rejected the

Reprinted from *The Spanish Tradition in America*, translated by Charles Gibson. Copyright © 1968 by Charles Gibson. Reprinted by permission of HarperCollins Publishers.

Spaniards' generosity, then the Spaniards after a reasonable interval could wage a just war against them.

In warfare it is proper that hostilities first be declared, so that barbarians may be admonished to accept the great benefits provided by the victor, to learn his best laws and customs, to familiarize themselves with the true religion, and to admit the sovereignity of the king of Spain. If they reject this sovereignity they may then be mistreated as enemies of the Spaniards, Spaniards who were sent by the king for the purpose of dominating them. If the barbarians request time to deliberate, they should be granted as much time as they need to summon a public meeting and make their decision, but they should not be allowed an excessive period of time. For if one has to wait while they deliberate on the nature, customs, and mentality of the Spaniards, and on their own, as well as on the differences between the two peoples, on the laws of government and of obedience, on the difference, honesty, and truth of morals and religion, then the time allowed would extend into infinity. Moreover it would all be in vain, for these matters cannot be known until after our rule has been accepted, through continuous contact with our people and with the teachings of those who instructed them in morality and religion.

If after being instructed in this way they obey our orders, they are then to be admitted into the faith. And they must be conceded the conditions of a just peace, so that, in the words of Deuteronomy (20:11) they shall be tributaries and they shall serve. But if they do not heed the warning, if they rashly reject the ambassadors, if they stubbornly refuse to take part in the conference, and if they prepare to resist, then on being defeated both they and their goods should fall to the hands of the victorious leader, to dispose of as he sees fit. To be sure, prudence and the cause of peace and of the public good should govern his decision, for these are considerations that he should always apply in punishing the enemy after the victory. Above all, he should avoid anything underhanded, so that they are not induced to error or to the desire or necessity of resisting through some ingenious trick. For unless everything is conducted in good faith, unless they clearly understand the admonitions and the claims made to them, fraud and malice serve only to obstruct justice. It is not justified in natural law, or in the

24

will and rule of a just prince, to admonish them negligently or to refuse to allow a period of time before making war. Such acts are unjust and they fall under the heading of robbery rather than war. . . . For if the barbarians are warned in advance they might then submit their possessions and persons to our sovereignty; and peace, which is the reason for making war, would then be achieved without fighting.

There are other particulars relating to the proper way of waging war, such as avoiding cupidity, cruelty, avarice, and wantonness. All these are alike in that they should be condemned as sins and disgraceful deeds, as St. Augustine says. If a war is undertaken for just causes and with the prince's authority, but if after being declared to the enemy it is waged in a malevolent spirit and with the object not of justice but of booty (which, as I said, is not free from disgrace and sin), even so, in the judgment of eminent theologians, the soldier's or chief's depraved will does not obligate a return of the booty won. It is the same as with an avaricious judge who condemns a traitor to be deprived of all his goods, for in this, though he acts for depraved and greedy ends, he inflicts a just punishment. It is not the depraved motive of the judge or soldier that causes the traitor or the enemy to be deprived of goods; it is rather the crime itself. The crime in the one case is injury to the monarchy; in the other it is injury to human society through an unjust war—for this crime is punished also in common legislation with capital punishment and loss of property. . . .

Turning then to our topic, whether it is proper and just that those who are superior and who excel in nature, customs, and laws rule over their inferiors, you can easily understand, if you are familiar with the character and moral code of the two peoples, that it is with perfect right that the Spaniards exercise their dominion over those barbarians of the New World and its adjacent islands. For in prudence, talent, and every kind of virtue and human sentiment they are as inferior to the Spaniards as children are to adults, or women to men, or the cruel and inhumane to the very gentle, or the excessively intemperate to the continent and moderate.

But I do not think that you expect me to speak of the prudence and talent of the Spaniards. . . . I refer simply to the princes and to those whose aid and skill they utilize to govern the state, to those, in short, who have received a liberal education. Because if a few individuals are unjust or wicked, this in itself does not mean that their turpitude tarnishes all their

25

people's reputation. A reputation should be measured in terms of cultivated and noble persons and their customs and public institutions, not in terms of depraved and serflike men whom their own nation is the first to despise. It is true that there are certain virtues to be esteemed in almost all the classes of our people, as for example valor, of which the Spanish legions through the course of history have given proofs that stagger human credulity. . . .

As for the Christian religion, I have witnessed many clear proofs of the firm roots it has in the hearts of Spaniards, even those dedicated to the military. The best proof of all has seemed to me to be the fact that in the great plague that followed the sack of Rome, in the Pontificate of Clement VII, not a single Spaniard among those who died in the epidemic failed to request in his will that all the goods stolen from the citizens be restored to them. And though there were many more Italians and Germans, no non-Spaniard, to my knowledge, fulfilled this obligation of the Christian religion. And I, who was following the army and was in the city observing it all diligently, was a witness to it. I recall that we have mentioned this in that Vatican meeting. What shall I say of the Spanish soldiers' gentleness and humanitarian sentiments? Their only and greatest solicitude and care in the battles, after the winning of the victory, is to save the greatest possible number of vanquished and free them from the cruelty of their allies. Now compare these qualities of prudence, skill, magnanimity, moderation, humanity, and religion with those of those little men [of America] in whom one can scarcely find any remnants of humanity. They not only lack culture but do not even use or know about writing or preserve records of their history—save for some obscure memory of certain deeds contained in painting. They lack written laws and their institutions and customs are barbaric. And as for their virtues, if you wish to be informed of their moderation and mildness, what can be expected of men committed to all kinds of passion and nefarious lewdness and of whom not a few are given to the eating of human flesh. Do not believe that their life before the coming of the Spaniards was one of Saturnine peace, of the kind that poets sang about. On the contrary, they made war with each other almost continuously, and with such fury that they considered a victory to be empty if they could not satisfy their prodigious hunger with the flesh of their enemies. This form of cruelty is especially prodigious among these people, remote as they are from the invincible ferocity of the Scythians, who also ate human bodies. But in other respects they are so cowardly and timid that they can scarcely offer any resistance to the hostile presence of our side, and many times thousands and thousands of them have been dispersed and have fled like women, on being defeated by a small Spanish force scarcely amounting to one hundred.

So as not to detain you longer in this matter, consider the nature of those people in one single instance and example, that of the Mexicans, who are regarded as the most prudent and courageous. Their king was Montezuma, whose empire extended the length and breadth of those regions and who inhabited the city of Mexico, a city situated in a vast lake, and a very well defended city both on account of the nature of its location and on account of its fortifications. It was similar to Venice, they say, but nearly three times as large both in extent and in population. Informed of the arrival of Cortés and of his victories and his intention to go to Mexico under pretext of a conference, Montezuma sought all possible means to divert him from his plan. Failing in this, terrorized and filled with fear, he received him in the city with about three hundred Spaniards. Cortés for his part, after taking possession of the city, held the people's cowardliness, ineptitude, and rudeness in such contempt that he not only compelled the king and his principal subjects, through terror, to receive the yoke and rule of the king of Spain, but also imprisoned King Montezuma himself, because of his suspicion that a plot was on foot to kill some Spaniards in a certain province. This he could do because of the stupor and inertia of the people, who were indifferent to the situation and preoccupied with other things than the taking up of arms to liberate their king. And thus Cortés, though aided by so small a number of Spaniards and so few natives, was able to hold them, oppressed and fearful at the beginning, for many days. They were so immense a multitude that he seemed lacking not only in discretion and prudence but even in common sense. Could there be a better or clearer testimony of the superiority that some men have over others in talent, skill, strength of spirit, and virtue? Is it not proof that they are slaves by nature? For the fact that some of them appear to have a talent for certain manual tasks is no argument for their greater human prudence. We see that certain insects, such as the bees and the spiders, produce works that no human skill can imitate. And as for the civil life of the inhabitants of New Spain and the province of Mexico, I have already said that the people are considered to be the most civilized of all. They themselves boast of their public institutions as if it were not a sufficient proof of their industry and civilization that they have rationally constructed cities, and kings appointed by popular suffrage rather than by hereditary right and age, and a commerce like that of civilized people. But see how they deceive themselves and how different is my opinion from theirs, since for me the foremost proof of the rudeness and barbarism and innate servitude of those people lies precisely in their public institutions, nearly all of which are servile and barbarous. They do have houses, and some rational mode of common life, and such commerce as natural necessity demands, but what does this prove other than that they are not bears or monkeys completely lacking in reason?

I have made reference to the customs and character of the barbarians. What shall I say now of the impious religion and wicked sacrifices of such people, who, in venerating the devil as if he were God, believed that the best sacrifice that they could placate him with was to offer him human hearts? And although this is all right if we understand by "hearts" the sound and pious souls of men, their practice was to use the expression not for the spirit that giveth life, to use St. Paul's words (2 Corinthians 3:6) but for the letter that killeth. And giving it a stupid and barbarous interpretation, they thought that they should sacrifice human victims. Opening up the human breasts they pulled out the hearts and offered them on their heinous altars. And believing that they had made a ritual sacrifice with which to placate their gods, they themselves ate the flesh of the victims. These are crimes that are considered by the philosophers to be among the most ferocious and abominable perversions, exceeding all human iniquity. And as for the fact that some nations, according to report, completely lack religion and knowledge of God, what else is this than to deny the existence of God and to live like beasts? In my judgment this crime is the most serious, infamous, and unnatural. The most shameful kind of idolatry is that of those who worship the belly and the lewdest organs of the body as if they were God, who make the pleasures of the body their religion and virtue, and who like pigs always have their eyes directed toward the ground, as if they had never seen the sky. For these especially the statement of St. Paul is applicable: "Whose end is destruction, whose God is their belly, and whose glory is their shame, who mind earthly things" (Philippians 3:19). How can we doubt that these people—so uncivilized, so barbaric, contaminated with so many impieties and obscenities—have been justly conquered by such an excellent, pious, and just king, as Ferdinand was and as the Emperor Charles is now, and by a nation excellent in every kind of virtue, with the best law and best benefit for the barbarians? Prior to the arrival of the Christians they had the nature, customs, religion, and practice of evil sacrifice as we have explained. Now, on receiving with our rule our writing, laws, and morality, imbued with the Christian religion, having shown themselves to be docile to the missionaries that we have sent them, as many have done, they are as different from their primitive condition as civilized people are from barbarians, or as those with sight from the blind, as the inhuman from the meek, as the pious from the impious, or to put it in a single phrase, in effect, as men from beasts.

QUESTIONS

1. Why does Sepúlveda consider the Indians of the Americas inferior?
2. Why are the Spaniards superior?
3. How do you think Sepúlveda has reached his conclusions in light of the fact that he had never been to the Americas?
4. How important do you think the duty to spread Christianity was to the Spaniards of the sixteenth century?

Scientific Revoluiton

READING

TO GOD THROUGH
THE STARS

Jonathan Spence

Jesuit missionaries looked at China with both awe and excitement, viewing its enormous population as a fertile field for religious conversion. Johann Adam Schall Von Bell (1591–1669) and Ferdinand Verbiest (1623–1688), like their Jesuit brothers before them, realized that the best way to accomplish their goals in a hierarchical society like China in the Ming (1368–1644) and Qing dynasties (1644–1911) was to adopt a strategy that would allow them access to those at the very top of the social ladder. They sought to do so by impressing Chinese officials with superior Western science and technology, which the missionaries hoped would lead to Chinese inquiries about Christianity.

Spence's article traces the careers of Schall and Verbiest to illustrate the consequences of an encounter between two cultures, each of which believed itself superior to the other. On one level, Schall's and Verbiest's experiences must have been thrilling, as each of them briefly established a close relationship with the emperor himself. On the other hand, they were forced to confront the fact that Chinese interest in science did not necessarily generate religious conversion. They found themselves in a quandary. When Schall and Verbiest began to rely more on their technological skills, they eventually became so busy that they sometimes neglected even their personal religious obligations. Their meteoric rise in the Chinese bureaucracy provided the

Reprinted from *To Change China: Western Advisors in China 1620–1960,* by permission of Viking Penguin, a division of Penguin Books (USA) Inc. Copyright © 1969 by Jonathan Spence.

potential to spread their beliefs among the literati, but it also ensnared them in the Chinese and Christian politics that eventually brought an end to the Jesuit mission.

———

On July 29, in the year 1644, Adam Schall, a Jesuit missionary residing in the city of Peking, sent a formal petition to the Emperor of China. "Your subject presents to Your Highness," wrote Schall, "predictions concerning an eclipse of the sun that will occur on September 1, 1644, calculated according to the new Western method, together with illustrations of the percentage of the solar eclipse, and the sun's reappearance as it may be seen in the Imperial capital and in various provinces. In some provinces the eclipse comes earlier, in others later. The predictive data are listed and presented for examination. Your subject humbly begs from Your Highness a decree to the Board of Rites to test publicly the accuracy of the predic-tion of the solar eclipse at a proper time."[1] Schall also offered to repair the astronomical instruments that had been damaged by a fire in the Palace the previous May. The Emperor ordered Schall to report for a public testing of his predictions at the beginning of September, and in the interim to pro-ceed with the casting of the new instruments.

The drama of that September confrontation comes clearly through the official Chinese report of the day's events: "On September 1, 1644, the grand secretary, Feng Ch'üan, was ordered in company with Adam Schall to bring the telescopes and other instruments to the observatory and to command the officials and students of the Calendrical Department and of the Bureau of Astronomy to repair to the observatory to study the eclipse of the sun. Only the prediction calculated by the Western method coin-cided exactly with the primary eclipse, the total eclipse, the passing of the eclipse, the time, the percentage, the location, and other details, whereas the predictions calculated by the [traditional Chinese] methods contained errors as to the time and percentage of the eclipse."[2] In recognition of his success, Schall was offered the directorship of the Bureau of Astronomy. This was an office of the fifth grade, placing the incumbent in the middle echelons of the nine-grade Chinese bureaucracy. After consultations with his Jesuit superiors, Schall accepted the post. The man of God became a Chinese bureaucrat.

This was no ordinary appointment. It was, rather, one of those rare moments in time when two streams of history converge, and the overtones of that convergence are to be the theme of our story. Before this moment China, secure in her superiority, had never dreamed that anything of value might be found in the West. The Chinese Empire was unquestionably the greatest in the world. The Chinese Emperor was the Son of Heaven, mediator between the spiritual and earthly realms, untouchable and unapproachable in the recesses of his glittering Court. What new techniques could be needed in a country that drew its wisdom from the Sages, controlled one hundred and fifty million subjects with a small and sophisticated bureaucracy, had touched perfection in art and in poetry, and plumbed the mysteries of sea, of earth, of sky? Civil wars, famines, even conquest by alien nomads such as Mongols or Manchus, were simply digressions; order would always be restored, the conquerors themselves would soon be subdued by the civilizing force of Chinese culture. For the Chinese, their country was "The Central Kingdom"; its boundaries were coterminous with "civilization." Those outside the boundaries were barbarians.

Though the Chinese could not conceivably be expected to have seen it—it was to take more than two centuries for the implications to become clear—Adam Schall was a portent. He came from a Europe that was experiencing a revolution in the fields of faith, knowledge and scientific technique. The Protestant Reformation had destroyed the Roman Catholic hegemony; the astronomical discoveries of Copernicus and Galileo, complementing Columbus's voyage to the Americas and Magellan's circumnavigation of the globe, shattered man's former vision of the earth, and the place of that earth in the universe. From the seventeenth century onward, the Chinese definition of the world was to come under increasing attack. The Westerners were not like earlier barbarians, who could be absorbed by China and learn to accept her values. Instead, their aim was to change China into something acceptable to them, to make China partake of Western values.[3]

Herein lies the significance of Adam Schall's appointment in 1644. For him, membership in the Chinese bureaucracy was not an end in itself: it was a means to a greater end, the conversion of the Chinese people to the Roman Catholic faith. Schall had developed his technical expertise, become an adviser to the Chinese, and finally their employee, all with the encouragement of his Jesuit superiors. Science was to be used to the greater glory of God. The Chinese, for their part, had favored and promoted Schall because it appeared that he might be useful to them as a technician, pure and simple. One side or the other had to fail in their designs.

Schall's presence in Peking, and the particular strategy that he had adopted, owed much to the activities of his Jesuit predecessor Matteo Ricci. Ricci had traveled to China in the late sixteenth century, and after years of frustration in attempting to convert the poor, had decided it would be more practical to win the favor of some Chinese officials or courtiers— to convert, in other words, from the top down. He accordingly concentrated on studying the Chinese *Classics,* so that he could converse with learned men on equal terms, and on demonstrating his prowess in the fields of mathematics, astronomy, cartography, and mechanics. As he had hoped, his skills aroused Chinese curiosity, and some of the curious became his backers. They used their influence on his behalf, and in 1601 Ricci was granted the exceptional favor of being permitted to live in Peking. Ricci discussed Roman Catholicism with Chinese scholars, and subtly pointed out that many of its main tenets could he found in the Confucian *Classics;* his great learning, and his personal probity, finally enabled him to convert several high-ranking officials to Christianity, and he secured permission to bring some more Jesuits to Peking.[4]

After Ricci died in 1610, his China journals were brought back to Europe by Father Nicolas Trigault, and rapidly went through several editions in Latin, French, Spanish, German, and Italian. Although there had been books on China before—such as Mendoza's *History* based on Spanish and Portuguese accounts[5]—Ricci's was the first to give a carefully written and reasoned description of the attainments of the great civilization on the other side of the earth. His readers learned not only that this China was indisputably the same as Marco Polo's Cathay, and that it was an exotic and colorful land where men ate their food with ivory sticks, drank an infusion of tea leaves, wore shoes of silk embroidered with flowers, and carried fans in the coldest weather; they were presented also with an analysis of a civilization that, despite its strength, might prove susceptible to Western influence. "I am of the opinion," wrote Ricci, "that the Chinese possess the ingenuous trait of preferring that which comes from without to that which they possess themselves, once they realize the superior quality of the foreign product. Their pride, it would seem, arises from an ignorance of the existence of higher things and from the fact that they find themselves far superior to the barbarous nations by which they are surrounded."[6]

The "foreign products" to which Ricci referred were such items as the clocks, the map, and the spinet which he had introduced to the Chinese Court; the "higher things," on the other hand, were the doctrines of Christianity, and it was going to be hard to convince the Chinese of the superiority of an alien religion. Ricci described the caution with which he and his fellow Jesuits had proceeded in this delicate field:

> In order that the appearance of a new religion might not arouse suspicion among the Chinese people, the Fathers did not speak openly about religious matters when they began to appear in public. What time was left to them, after paying their respects and civil compliments and courteously receiving their visitors, was spent in studying the language of the country, the methods of writing and the customs of the people. They did, however, endeavor to teach this pagan people in a more direct way, namely, by virtue of their example and by the sanctity of their lives. In this way they attempted to win the goodwill of the people and little by little, without affectation, to dispose their minds to receive what they could not be persuaded to accept by word of mouth, without endangering what had been thus far accomplished.[7]

This language must have rung oddly in the ears of European readers attuned to the rigors of the Inquisition and Counter-Reformation, but nevertheless many of them were intrigued.

One who listened was Johann Adam Schall von Bell. Born into a wealthy and noble Cologne family, Schall had entered the Jesuit order in 1611, at nineteen, and was studying in Rome when Trigault arrived there on his mission. The two men met. Schall was convinced by the posthumous message of Ricci that he had found his true vocation; he applied for permission to serve his God in the Far East and it was granted. . . .

In Lisbon Schall joined twenty-one Jesuits who had been selected for China service, 614 other passengers and crew, and some ten thousand live poultry, on the ship *Nossa Senhora de Jesus.* They sailed on April 16, 1618, and despite the fact that they were "stowed like herrings among the goods, luggage and provisions," training for the future started as soon as they were on the open sea. Under Trigault's direction they pursued their studies: mathematics on Tuesdays and Fridays, the Chinese language on Wednesdays and Saturdays. In addition, Schall was one of a small group who worked at astronomy, since his superiors had noted Ricci's recommendation that if the Jesuits could attain the skills necessary for correcting the Chinese calendar "this would enhance our reputation, give us freer entry into China and secure us greater security and liberty."[8]

Schall's vessel reached Goa on the western Indian coast on October 4, 1618. The five and a half months' voyage had been costly. Forty-five of the passengers had died from fever, among them five of the Jesuits. Two more Jesuits still in a weakened state died in Goa. Here the surviving passengers learned for the first time that in 1616 the Jesuits living in China had been arrested and ordered to leave China forever, their church and residence in Nanking had been razed, and Christianity formally banned. Fortunately the orders had not been forcefully pushed through, and several Jesuits had stayed on, hidden by Chinese converts, both in Peking and the provinces.[9]

Schall and the others determined to press on, and finally reached Portuguese Macao on July 15, 1619. In Macao, Schall was once again put to work at the Chinese language, this time under the direction of Father Valignoni who had been expelled from China during the persecutions. He was still there in June 1622, when the Dutch attacked the Portuguese settlement and were beaten off, partly by the accuracy of a cannon fired from the Jesuit residence. Sometime in the late summer Schall and three other Jesuits crossed quietly into China and set out for the north. Leaving the party in Hangchow, Schall joined Father Longobardi, who had remained in hiding during the persecution, and on January 25, 1623, the two men entered Peking, taking up residence in the small house near the southwest city gate where Ricci once had lived.[10]

Schall described their arrival as follows: "I remember how while still a young man, I accompanied the aged Father Longobardi to Peking. He and another father presented a petition to the Emperor, in which they said simply that they wished to stay in the capital to work on the bronze cannon."[11] Though the fathers still technically under the ban of expulsion received no reply, added Schall, they stayed on in Peking on the pretext of awaiting an Imperial edict granting them permission. Behind these curious proceedings lay the fact that certain important changes in the Chinese political scene had occurred which indirectly favored the Jesuits. Shen Ch'üeh, the official who had been responsible for launching the 1616 persecution, was briefly out of favor; and in 1621 Manchu tribesmen, north of the Great Wall, had inflicted severe defeats on the Ming armies. This gave influential Chinese officials, among them the Christian converts Hsü Kuang-ch'i and Li Chih-tsao, the chance to bring the Westerners' technical accomplishments to the embattled Ming Emperor's attention. They urged that cannon be brought from Macao to be used against the Manchus in the north, and suggested that the Jesuits be employed as advisers. The cannon arrived, but unfortunately two of them exploded, killing several Chinese bystanders, and Shen Ch'üeh used this incident to renew his attacks on the Christians, though unable to get them again expelled from Peking, or to prevent them preaching in the provinces.[12]

While the Ming dynasty fought for survival on its frontiers, and in the capital a ruthless eunuch and his faction struggled for power with reformers in the Confucian bureaucracy,[13] Schall followed Ricci's advice and calmly began his astronomical work. Astronomy and calendrical science had great politico-religious importance in China, since the Emperor was regarded as the mediator between heaven and earth, and the calendars issued in his name were followed unswervingly both in China and the tributary states on her borders. Throughout the vast Chinese Empire sowing and harvest, festivals and funerals, political decisions and judicial assizes, almost all facets of life ran to the rhythm of the lunar months and auspicious days recorded by Peking. Errors in the calendar accordingly took on a portentous significance, and in times of dynastic weakness they could call in question the Emperor's right to the title Son of Heaven. If the Jesuits could only prove that Chinese calendrical science was inaccurate, they would gain great prestige. To reassure critics in Europe who were ignorant of this background, and protested that too much time was spent in such occupations, Schall wrote: "There is nothing surprising in the fact

37

that the Jesuits apply all their energies to the reform of astronomy, since it is purely scientific occupation, not at all out of place for religious men."[14] What he meant by this was that though it was, of course, surprising for a missionary to be devoting all his efforts to astronomy, it seemed to be the sole channel through which the Chinese could be brought to God. For only if the Jesuits earned official appointments through their technical abilities could they hope to be brought into the Imperial bureaucracy; this would win them the friendship of influential Chinese scholars, and give them the power and the opportunity to make mass conversions.

Schall established his reputation by correctly predicting the eclipse of October 8, 1623. The effect of this was heightened when he predicted the eclipse of September 1625, and wrote his first book in Chinese no astronomy, which he disarmingly described as "a little treatise on eclipses, in two sections, which I composed to practice my Chinese writing style during my first stay in the Imperial City." In 1626 he produced a Chinese treatise on the telescope, concentrating on its useful to astronomy, but not neglecting to point out that it could also be useful in time of war.[15]

Though Schall's skills were gaining him important contacts in Peking officialdom, in 1627 his Jesuit superiors posted him to the northwestern province of Shensi. . . .

Despite his inexperience, Schall threw himself into his new task with his customary energy, and by 1629 he had made friends with several local officials, baptized numerous converts, and succeeded in erecting a fine church topped with a golden cross in the provincial capital of Sian.[16] But Schall had no chance to follow up these initial successes, for in 1630 he was abruptly summoned back to Peking.

In his absence Hsü Kuang-ch'i, the Christian convert and staunch supporter of the Jesuits, had been made a vice-president of the Board of Rites, a position near the summit of the Imperial bureaucracy, and in 1629 he had proved successfully that the Western methods of astronomical calculation were superior to those of the Chinese and Mohammedan astronomers presently employed by the Court. He was ordered to head a newly formed Calendrical Department and to staff it as he wished. He selected his friend and fellow convert Li Chih-tsao and the two Jesuits Longobardi and Terrentius.[17] Here was the first chance of a toehold in the official bureaucracy for which the Jesuits had waited. Terrentius (Johann Schreck), a brilliant astronomer and mathematician, had been a member of the Cesi Academy with Galileo. Understandably upset by the Pope's 1616 injunction forbidding him to defend the Copernican heliocentric theories, Galileo had refused to give the Jesuits help in predicting eclipses. But Terrentius was in regular correspondence with Kepler, the other great European astronomer of the time, and thus eminently qualified to attempt a synthesis of available knowledge and to lead the Jesuits to a position of dominance in the Chinese technical bureaus.

Jesuit hopes for such triumphs received a setback when Terrentius died suddenly in 1630. Schall was recalled from Shensi to take his place. Though not as great a mathematician as Terrentius, Schall's knowledge of Western astronomy was enough to put him far ahead of the Chinese and Mohammedan opposition. He had at his fingertips the latest techniques, fruits of the European revolution in the sciences: new methods for predicting eclipses, geometrical analyses of planetary motion, the concepts of a spherical earth and the division of its surface by meridians and parallels, advanced algebra, and such aids to precision as the telescope and the micrometer screw.[18] Thus it didn't really matter that because of Church dogma the Jesuits didn't bring the most developed heliocentric theories to China; they already had the technical edge over the Chinese.

Taking up work where Terrentius had left off, Schall set about examining the Chinese astronomical calculations and found them wanting: "In the Chinese ephemerides, vulgarly called a calendar," he wrote, "we found an 'alternative' placed beside almost every day, which didn't please us much; and in the other calendar used to show the planetary motions we noticed right away a large number of mistakes which stemmed from their faulty calculations." Accordingly he resolved to offer the throne "a complete astronomy book"; he worked five years on it, producing a work in three parts, one on planetary theory, one on fixed stars, and one of tables to aid calculation.[19] Unfortunately his superior and protector, Hsü Kuang-ch'i, died in 1633. Schall, never very tolerant of human frailty, was ill at ease under the new director, Li T'ien-ching. "Li was a fine man," wrote Schall in one of his terse pen-portraits, "but too peace-loving, and in those areas where he should have fought a bit he yielded." "Those areas" were virtually the whole field of calendrical calculation and astronomical observation; under Li's direction there was incessant squabbling among conflicting factions in the bureau. Schall had to fight constantly in defense of his own methods, and to preserve his independence, since "I knew perfectly well that the moment the Chinese mathematicians got involved my projects would come to nothing." Somehow he still found time to deal with problems of hydraulics and optics, and even to repair the spinet that Ricci had long before given to the Wan-li Emperor. For good measure he wrote out—in Chinese—a complete guide to spinet-playing.[20]

Taking advantage of the entrée to the Court that the repair of the spinet had afforded him, Schall offered the Emperor two gifts which he had brought from Europe with him in 1618 but never before had had a chance to present. One was an illuminated life of Christ, on fine parchment, to which he had added a Chinese commentary; the other, a representation in wax of the adoration of the Magi, finely colored. The Emperor accepted the gifts, and was reported to be delighted with them. Schall did not see the Emperor in person—such opportunities were only to come after his 1644 promotion into the Chinese bureaucracy—but in the palace negotiations that preceded the presentations he was able to meet some of the Court eunuchs and to convert them. These eunuchs, at Schall's bidding, carried the Christian message into the forbidden quarters of the Emperor's palace. Here lived the Emperor's wives and concubines, with whom only the Emperor and castrated males might converse; some of these palace women were in fact converted, though it hardly seems possible that they received sophisticated teaching from their recently converted eunuch associates. Nevertheless, Schall felt that such roundabout tactics were justified, since one never knew which favored concubine might not bring the Emperor himself to see the light. He pointed out, to a possibly skeptical European audience, that God's grace was clearly manifest in these transactions: Chinese concubines grew more beautiful and rose in the palace hierarchy after baptism, while those who mocked God's word developed unsightly blemishes, and fell from favor.[21]

All this shows the ambiguity of Schall's position. He was sure of his superiority over the Chinese technicians, but was constantly having to prove it. He was convinced of the truth of his own religion, yet at the same time he knew that the Chinese considered their own civilization far superior to his. He hoped ultimately to convert the Emperor, but was barred from his presence and had to use eunuchs as his spiritual intermediaries, making exaggerated claims for their few successes. At times the dynamic missionary was transmuted by the heavy confidence of the Chinese into an artisan and errand boy. Members of the bureaucracy, whose conversion he also richly desired, shrewdly gauged his waxing or waning influence.

Schall had learned from Matteo Ricci, and confirmed through his own experience, that the Confucian bureaucrats were a well-educated elite, proud of their sophistication. Methods of conversion that had been successful in the ruder societies of Latin America or Southeast Asia would not work in China. Thus, though Schall was a forthright man, he was horrified by the brash tactics of two Franciscan friars who appeared in Peking in 1637. . . .

Unlike the eager friars, Schall followed contemporary Jesuit theory and did as little as possible to upset the members of the Confucian elite or to disturb their existing beliefs. The quickest way to achieve conversion in China would be conversion from the top; to succeed, he must do the Emperor's bidding at all times and gain the respect of the Chinese who mattered. Schall therefore endeavored to live like a Confucian official. He worked hard at the Chinese language, studied the Confucian *Classics,* wore the long robes of the Chinese scholar, and lived in considerable style. To translate the word "God" he used accepted terms for "Deity" and "Lord of Heaven" culled from the Chinese literary heritage, assuring his European critics that there were theistic elements in the Confucian canon that made such usage legitimate. Furthermore, he accepted the idea that the rites which the Chinese performed in honor of their ancestors or of Confucius had purely civil significance, and that Chinese converts to Christianity might continue to practice such rites without being condemned as heretical.

By these methods Schall and his fellow Jesuits were able to gain the confidence of influential Chinese, and had made several thousand converts in China by 1640, including fifty palace women, forty eunuchs and over one hundred others in the Emperor's entourage.[22] It seemed that finally Schall was breaking through to the Emperor himself. His presents had been accepted, his astronomy praised, and he was given new and important duties. The threats of war from the Manchu tribes, now united and organized into a hostile state on China's northern frontiers, led the Emperor to issue an edict in 1642 ordering Schall to devote his energies to the casting of cannon for use in campaigns against the Manchus.

Schall protested that he only had a book knowledge of cannon-making; nonetheless, he was given an open area of land, supplies and laborers, and told to get on with the job. The work was simple enough, Schall found, commenting rather contemptuously that "all these things which are quite ordinary to Europeans seem extraordinary to the Chinese who have no experience of them."[23] The commission brought him the status of a mandarin and commensurate power over his underlings. Taking advantage of this, he ordered his workers to kneel at an altar in the foundry before starting work. After twenty large cannon had been successfully cast, he was ordered by the Emperor to make another five hundred, each weighing only sixty pounds, to be carried by infantry soldiers into action. Schall noted caustically that such cannon would inevitably be abandoned by the fleeing Chinese troops and fall into Manchu hands. Presumably he kept his scepticism to himself, since his military advice was increasingly sought; in 1643 he was ordered to submit designs for improved fortifications in Peking, and in 1644 was sent to check the northern defenses. He reported that the situation appeared hopeless.[24]

The situation was indeed hopeless, and Schall had to stand by as the bandit army of Li Tzu-ch'eng swept into Peking in April 1644 with fire and sword, and the Ming Emperor committed suicide in his palace. It must have seemed to Schall that his whole life's work was going up in the flames of the burning city. For twenty-one years he had been at the bidding of the Ming Emperor and labored to impress the Ming bureaucracy. Now the dynasty had been overthrown, and he and the other Jesuits would have to start again. But Schall was not one to give up easily. The first priority was to protect his property from the looters who roamed the streets. . . .

The second priority was to get in touch with Li Tzu-ch'eng, since even if he was a bandit, he was also the leader of a victorious army, and there was always the chance that he might prove to be the founder of a new dynasty. So Schall reported to the bandit leader's palace and was granted a long interview; presumably he offered his services, but he gives us no record of what transpired, save that the meeting was cordial and he was offered wine and food.[25]

Li Tzu-ch'eng in turn was routed by the Manchu armies from the north, and Schall seems for the first time to have called in question the whole Jesuit strategy of conversion through technical work. "I had already taken the decision," he wrote, "to abandon the calendar and astronomy in order to concern myself solely with religion." He must have felt that the Ming overthrow was God's warning to him personally. But when Li Tzu-ch'eng's soldiers, fleeing from the Manchus, set fire to the area in which

Schall lived, the house where he had stored all his mathematical books was spared, although the leaves of the trees all around it were scorched and burnt. Schall seized on this as renewed evidence of God's blessing: "I could not stop myself thinking that such an extraordinary action of fire on such dry materials must be a good augury."[26] So in June, when the Manchus had consolidated their hold on the city, he offered them his services.

Schall's position was a strong one. The Manchus had founded the Ch'ing dynasty and were anxious to consolidate their claims as the holders of the Mandate of Heaven, the true heirs to the Ming. To do this, they had to prepare accurate calendars and predictions on the Chinese model, and prove they were not simply northern barbarians. Schall's work in the Calendrical Department was well known. His two main rivals were the Ming and the Mohammedan astronomers, but he had already proved that his expertise was greater than theirs, and as a Westerner he was a free agent, owing no loyalties to the defeated dynasty. Fully aware of this, Schall had even had the temerity to petition the Manchus for continuation of his special privilege of living in Peking, since he was "a foreigner like you," and his petition had been granted.[27] It was at this point that he threw out the challenge to the rival schools of astronomy and forced them to a direct confrontation. The Manchu Emperor accepted the evidence of Schall's superior skills and made him director of the Bureau of Astronomy.

Now that Schall had become an established official in the Ch'ing bureaucracy he had to make the most of his new position, and he did so in a number of ways. He performed feats of astronomical calculation and mechanical expertise which, at little cost, boosted his own image. He accompanied his official astronomical pronouncements with moralistic observations calculated to curb the young Emperor's sexual excesses and errors of judgment.[28] His fame could be brought to aid fellow missionaries: "Throughout the Empire my name was so spread that almost all knew of me. It was often useful to my companions, situated elsewhere, to say they were my brothers or friends."[29] He acted as the interpreter for foreign envoys arriving at the capital, even if, like the Dutch, they were enemies of his faith. "The upshot was," Schall wrote, "that if something occurred that no one dared to handle, the courtiers said 'Let Father Adam deal with it.'"[30]

The purpose of all this activity was, once again, to speed the conversion of the Chinese people. In the early years of the Ch'ing dynasty Schall was on good terms with senior Chinese officials, Manchu generals and princes, and in contact with many women of the palace including the Dowager Empress. But as always, progress was frustratingly slow. As he wrote to a friend in 1651: "To sum up in a word what I think of the Tartars—they are not yet sated with rape and murder, and have not yet abandoned lewdness in shamefully abusing their captives. I live amongst them, I have daily dealings with them. Very often I offer them the doctrine of salvation, but I have to beware of casting my pearls before swine; not, I should add, just to those who seem totally hostile, but even to those I think ready to receive it. Nevertheless, I get nowhere."[31] It was not until the mid-1650's that he began to draw near to the greatest and most elusive prize, the Emperor himself.

The regent Dorgon, who had been de facto ruler for the boy Emperor, died in 1650, and in 1651 the Shun-chih Emperor, now thirteen years old, took the reins of government in person and carried out an extensive purge of Dorgon's henchmen. He seems to have truly admired and trusted Schall, whom he called *ma-fa* (grandfather), constantly waiving palace etiquette on his behalf. Schall was excused from the customary prostrations, given Imperial permission to adopt a son (Shun-chih was distressed that the celibate Schall had no heir), permitted to hand over his official memorials in person, granted land on which to build a church in Peking, and allowed to sit in the Imperial presence. He was given an honorary title of the first rank which placed him in the top echelons of the Ch'ing bureaucracy, and his ancestors were posthumously ennobled.[32] Schall claims that at the peak of his favor, in 1656–1657, Shun-chih visited his house on twenty-four occasions, often unannounced, and talked with him informally late into the night. They discussed astronomy, government, the Christian religion, and much else; Schall was struck by the young Emperor's intelligence and eagerness to learn, and felt they shared a mutual esteem, yet conversion never came. As Schall wrote sadly, "most men, especially these orientals, hold deep in their hearts something that faith in God has as yet been unable to remove." In Shun-chih's case the greatest barrier was chastity, or rather, monogamy; he couldn't answer Schall's subtle question of why it was that European husbands with one wife should often have more children than a Chinese with ten concubines, but he still showed no inclination to give up his luxurious palace life. He also remained an inflexible determinist, convinced that the stars in their courses controlled his destiny.[33]

Perhaps Schall's insistence began to weary Shun-chih. Certainly by 1658 he was spending less time with Schall and more with a small group of Buddhist monks who had won his confidence.[34] Old and disappointed, Schall found that these balmy years had been but a brief respite, and he became once more "a skiff in mid-ocean," as he put it.[35] His enemies took the opportunity to close in.

These enemies were of two kinds, Chinese astronomers and Catholic missionaries. Though the astronomers brought his downfall, it was the missionaries who first gave him trouble. At issue was Schall's whole policy of cultural adaptation. It was not merely that he lived like the Chinese: a European visitor to Peking in the 1650's described him as being "shaved and clothed after the Tartar fashion," and "carried by four men in a Palakin or Sedan, attended by several considerable persons on Horse-back."[36] To many, he seemed also to think like the Chinese, and to be far too tolerant of their pagan rites. His policies had serious theological overtones, and even fellow Jesuits thought he was making too many concessions. Furthermore, Schall was often intemperate and moody: "on the exterior a rather harsh man, very irascible and morose after the German fashion," wrote one contemporary.[37]

Dominicans and Franciscans, who were entering China in some numbers and believed in a life of poverty and conversion of the poor, were often jealous of the Jesuits' influence, and attacked both the Jesuits' religious position and their lavish style of life. Owing to their protests, the Jesuit practices were condemned by the Archbishop of Manila in 1635, and in 1645 the Pope issued his own prohibition. Another condemnation was handed down by a committee of five theologians of the Roman College in 1655. The Jesuits marshaled their defenses, and persuaded the Pope to withdraw the prohibition in 1656; this prompted the Dominicans to return to the attack with renewed vigor.[38]

All this controversy placed Schall in an awkward position, especially as many of these friars also condemned his work in the astronomical bureau as beings grossly superstitious. "The case was," wrote one Dominican who was in Peking with Schall, "that Father Adam being president of the

College of Mathematics, had the charge of, as well in Political as Religious respects, assigning lucky and unlucky Days for every thing they are to do (tho some excused the said Father as to this particular)." He summarized Schall's duties as being to choose "days and hours for everything except eating, drinking, and sinning."[39] A Franciscan gave even broader criticisms: "The Jesuits have selected purely human means to spread the faith, in direct contradiction to the means used by the Apostles, recommended by Christ Our Lord, and employed by all those who subsequently worked to spread the Kingdom of God—with the exception of said Jesuit Fathers. Using their own means the Jesuits in the Oriental missions set themselves before the heathen as men of wealth and influence, even as men of power and nobility. From this it follows that they are unwilling to allow missionaries of other orders to enter the territories in which they are preaching, lest the heathen, after seeing these obedient, poor and humble men, should turn against the Jesuits who would be shamed and confounded."[40]

Schall could have ridden out these storms with his customary bravado, but he was unable to handle the persistent hostility of the scholar-astronomer Yang Kuang-hsien, who became the spokesman for the anti-Christian literati. The tempo of the attack increased after Shun-chih died in 1661. Schall's Chinese adversaries finally resorted to the accusation of high treason. As they memorialized in 1664:

> The Westerner Adam Schall was a posthumous follower of Jesus, who had been the ringleader of the treacherous bandits of the Kingdom of Judea. In the Ming dynasty he came to Peking secretly, and posed as a calendar-maker in order to carry on the propagation of heresy. He engaged in spying out the secrets of our court. If the Westerners do not have intrigues within and without China, why do they establish Catholic churches both in the capital and in strategic places in the provinces? During the last twenty years they have won over one million disciples who have spread throughout the Empire. What is their purpose? Evidently they have long prepared for rebellion. If we do not eradicate them soon, then we ourselves rear a tiger that will lead us to future disaster.[41]

The charges were investigated, and though Schall with the aid of the newly arrived Jesuit Ferdinand Verbiest was able to prove that he was innocent of astronomical errors, he was found guilty on the other charges and sentenced to death by dismemberment. Because of his age, this sentence was altered to flogging and banishment, and even those punishments were not carried out because of his meritorious services in the past. Instead, Schall, partially paralyzed and unable to speak as the result of a stroke, was allowed to stay on under house arrest in his Peking residence. He died there peacefully in 1666, at the age of seventy-five. But Catholicism was proscribed, the churches were closed, and the other missionaries banished to Macao and Canton. Many of them had not regretted Schall's fall. Two jokes popular in Macao at this time summarize their attitudes: "One Adam having driven us out of Paradise, another has driven us out of China"; "Father Ricci got us into China with his mathematics, and Father Schall got us out with his."[42]

Schall could forgive his Chinese persecutors on the grounds of his own interpretation of their national character: "Such is the desire for vengeance among the Chinese, a passion so inordinate that, even amidst public disasters, the ineffaceable memory of what they consider an affront, and the tenacious rancor of their private hatreds, leads them to forget themselves as long as they might bring harm to others."[43] He found it harder to forgive those of his own faith and background whom he considered too narrow-minded and shortsighted to see the point of what he was doing. "I thought to myself of all the work that for over twenty years I had given to the reform of astronomy, and I wished that it should not be lost. For it was to astronomy that I was indebted and I hoped for similar results for my successors. At the same time I saw to my great sorrow that this work was held in contempt by those who above all should have encouraged it."[44] There could be no clearer summary of the way that Adam Schall, man of God, had been edged aside by Adam Schall, Chinese astronomer.

. . . Ferdinand Verbiest was born in 1623, the son of a bailiff on a great estate in western Flanders. He was educated in Jesuit schools in Courtrai and Bruges, and entered the order in 1641. After some years of teaching grammar, Greek, and rhetoric at Brussels, he was sent to complete advanced studies in theology at Seville and Rome. A brilliant intellectual, enjoying the confidence of his superiors, he could have looked forward to a distinguished life in the highest circles of Catholic Europe. Instead, from an early age, he badgered the General of the Order for a posting to a foreign mission. His requests were all firmly turned down until finally in 1655 his tenacity bore fruit. "I approve your praiseworthy desires," wrote the Jesuit General Goswin Nickel, "I hope that they will be realized, and that your entry into China will bring salvation to the souls of many."[45]

After pirates had rudely interrupted his first journey, Verbiest made his way to Lisbon and sailed for the Far East in the spring of 1657, reaching Goa in the autumn and Macao the following summer. Early in 1659 the Chinese authorities allowed him to enter China, and he took up his missionary duties in Sian, Shensi province, where Schall had worked thirty years before. For eight months Verbiest labored, apparently with success, though as yet he was not an expert at the Chinese language; then in February 1660 the Shun-chih Emperor summoned him to Peking, to assist Schall in his astronomical work. Verbiest lived in China for a further twenty-eight years, but he was never again to work simply as a missionary among the Chinese people. Like Schall, his energies were to be absorbed by the world of science and the Court of the Emperor.

The first real test of Verbiest's astronomical ability came during the persecutions of 1664, and he acquitted himself well. Ordered by the tribunal to estimate the exact time of a forthcoming eclipse of the sun, the Chinese astronomer Yang Kuang-hsien estimated 2:15, the Mohammedan astronomer Wu Ming-hsüan 2:30, while Verbiest with the help of the stricken Schall, claimed it would not occur till 3 o'clock. Lenses had been set up so that the sun's image was projected into a dark room—the first two calculations having proved erroneous, almost exactly at 3 o'clock the first shadow appeared. This triumph was not enough to sway the judges, and Verbiest was condemned to flogging and banishment. However, this punishment and Schall's sentence of execution were both commuted, and the two were allowed to stay on together under house arrest in Peking, though now they had no official position, and their enemy Yang Kuang-hsien had been appointed director of the astronomical bureau.[46]

48

After Schall's death in 1666, Verbiest was still under house arrest. Feeling that Schall, despite his setbacks, had been on the right track, Verbiest devoted his enforced leisure to astronomical studies; as he wrote in a letter dated April 1668, "instead of earthly news I send herewith news of the Heavens."[47] He was waiting for the political situation to change and when it did he moved fast and effectively.

By late 1668 Emperor Shun-chih's son K'ang-hsi, now fourteen, had taken over the throne in person, punishing his regents and their followers for their excesses. At the same time it was becoming apparent that the calculations made by Yang Kuang-hsien and Wu Ming-hsüan in the astronomical bureau were often inaccurate. In December, repeating Schall's move of 1644, Verbiest challenged the two astronomers to prove their skill by calculating the length of the shadow that would be thrown by a given object at a given time of day. Yang and Wu were unable to complete the experiment, but Verbiest's calculations proved exact. Then on December 28, Verbiest received an order from K'ang-hsi to check the calendars that his rivals had submitted. At the end of January 1669 Verbiest replied, pointing out several major errors that had been made by the Chinese and Mohammedan astronomers; he ended with a broad-based summary of the role of the calendar in China. It is hard to remember that this is a Belgian Jesuit, not a Chinese official, speaking: "The virtue and the power of our Imperial Majesty has spread far and wide, so that many scores of nations are tribute-bearers and the nations which follow our Imperial calendars extend for several myriads of miles. From the Imperial Capital of our Empire the authority radiates to the four corners of the earth. In such an immense territory how can we endure an inaccurate calendar that can nowhere measure the real length of day and night, the correct time, or the real solar periods all year round?"[48]

The Emperor ordered the princes and senior ministers to investigate Verbiest's charges and submit a report on their findings. The ministers replied that Verbiest seemed to have been right and Wu Ming-hsüan wrong. The K'ang-hsi Emperor found this conclusion too vague, and issued an angry edict which showed that he intended to settle these astronomical squabbles once and for all:

49

Earlier when Yang Kuang-hsien accused Schall, the princes and ministers in the state-council determined clearly on what points Yang Kuang-hsien was right and accordingly approved his suggestions, and on what points Schall was wrong, and accordingly considered how to discontinue his calculations. You have not now carefully investigated why formerly the state-council decided to abolish the Western method nor why you now decide to restore it without further investigation of Ma Hu, Yang Kuang-hsien, Wu Ming-hsüan and Verbiest before memorializing to Us. This is improper. We order you to deliberate this matter again![49]

Verbiest and Wu Ming-hsüan were ordered to carry out a final round of competitive experiments, by calculating the precise height and angle of the sun as it would appear at a given time. All instruments had to be in place two weeks early, and the astronomers then fixed them in position, and covered the movable parts with strips of paper on which they laid the imprint of their personal seals. Thus it was impossible to tamper with the forecasts. Verbiest's calculations proved precise, and in late February 1669 he was appointed director of the astronomical bureau. Yang Kuang-hsien and Wu Ming-hsüan were arrested.

. . . This success, however, was as paradoxical for Verbiest as it had been for Schall: increasing technical duties deflected him from his spiritual endeavors. He not only had little time to convert the heathen, he even had to give up his personal devotions. As he wrote in August 1670 to his closest friend Philippe Couplet: "Last year I hoped that the pressure of business would gradually decline as the months passed, but I am still overwhelmed with work, to the point that the Father Superior has to dispense me—and this has not been a rare occurrence—from reciting my breviary."[50]

Verbiest worked on the calendars, directed his bureau staff, and built large and complex instruments for the Imperial observatory;[51] but the "pressure of business" to which he referred was not entirely due to the demands of astronomy. Much of his time was taken up with trivia. At the K'ang-hsi Emperor's request he spent weeks on end perfecting a system of pulleys to lever giant stones over a rickety bridge, making gay sundials and a water clock, building pumps to raise the water in the royal pleasure gardens, and painting tiny trompe l'oeil figures to be viewed through a prismatic

50

tube. Verbiest described one such object, a little landscape, with horses and birds in the foreground, which could be enjoyed as a painting in its own right. "But when viewed through a prismatic tube, one could see in it only a tartar's head and body, down to the belt, dressed in robe and summer hat. All were amused at seeing this image."[52] He was proud of these activities, and described them at length in his letters, for of course these activities would turn out not to have been trivial if they led to the supreme goal—conversion of the Emperor. Verbiest was optimistic that the K'ang-hsi Emperor, having been impressed by astronomy and delighted by mechanics, would swing to the faith behind the science. "Thanks to Divine Providence we hope that this [Imperial] favor will grow, and will finally bring our joy to a peak. But we must still be patient, wait for the suitable moment, moving little by little along the way which will lead to the difficult and important goal."[53] So Schall had hoped and waited for his Emperor.

But like Schall, Verbiest also had his enemies. These included Jesuits in Peking, many years his senior, who resented his growing prestige. When Verbiest asked his superiors in Europe for more money to meet the costs of his scientific establishment and the inevitable payments and bribes of life at the Manchu court, he wrote in Flemish so that other Jesuits would be unable to read his letter. He was convinced that he was on the right track, and determined that his colleagues should not thwart him: "All the favors that we have obtained up to now have been given by the Emperor as payment for services rendered in the field of mathematics. Right there is sufficient reason to let me continue and to give me resources."[54]

Verbiest's knowledge of Chinese grew good enough for him to act as interpreter for visiting foreigners. When the K'ang-hsi Emperor ordered him to the palace to serve as his tutor, Verbiest also learned Manchu so that they could converse informally, and finally wrote a Manchu grammar to help other missionaries in learning the language. Under his direction K'ang-hsi studied the principles of astronomy, worked through the *Elements of Euclid* (which Ricci had translated into Chinese long before), moved on to spherical trigonometry, and finally to practical experiments in astronomical observation and terrestrial measurement.[55]

How close the two men really were, and how much of this new knowledge K'ang-hsi comprehended, is a moot point. Verbiest wrote of the Emperor's intelligence and the affection between them, while other missionaries believed that the Emperor followed little of what was going on.[56]

But certainly some real personal contact took place, and new assignments and rewards came to Verbiest. An edict of 1674 ordered him to cast "light but effective cannons, convenient for transportation" to be used in the suppression of the civil war that had erupted in South China.[57] Verbiest made 132 heavy cannon; their success in the field brought an order for 320 light cannon. In 1682, with victory assured to the Imperial forces, Verbiest was given the title of vice-president of the Board of Works, because "the cannons whose casting he had directed were good and strong."[58] The bailiffs son from Flanders had become a senior member of the Chinese bureaucracy.

Favor and obligation naturally overlapped. Thus Verbiest, chosen by the Emperor to accompany him on one of his Imperial tours to Manchuria, described his role as follows: "I was to be always at the Emperor's side, so that I might make in his presence the necessary observations for determining the state of the heavens, the elevation of the Pole, the grade of the terrain, and to calculate with my mathematical instruments the height and distance of the mountains. He could also conveniently ask me to tell him about meteorites, and any other problems of physics or mathematics."[59] Verbiest was given ten horses to carry the equipment and lodged each night in a tent near the Emperor's. Choked by the dust of the marching army, exhausted by each day's hard riding so that "during the trip I was so tired each night on reaching my tent that I could not stand upright," there was no respite for Verbiest from the honors he had earned: "I would have excused myself several times from following the Emperor, had not my friends advised me to the contrary and had I not feared that the Emperor might notice my absence and take it badly."[60]

This tenacity brought its small rewards, as on one night in the mountains when a chosen group sat with the Emperor at the edge of a stream. Verbiest describes the scene: "As it was a beautiful night, and the sky was clear, K'ang-hsi asked me to give him the Chinese and European names for the stars appearing on the horizon; he himself named first those that he had already learned. Then, taking out a little celestial map that I had given him some years before, he began to calculate from the stars what hour of night it was, taking great pleasure in showing those around how much skill he had acquired in science."[61]

Such moments kept Verbiest's hopes of conversion alive as other business pressed upon him. Not only did he continue with astronomical writing, preparing tables "for 2,000 years into the future" at K'ang-hsi's request, he drew up new tables of the latitudes of cities in Manchuria which K'ang-hsi ordered adopted in all future Chinese maps.[62] As vice-provincial of the order in China he worked for all missionaries; Franciscan friars, for example, repeatedly praised his disinterested help and the influence he could bring to bear to save them from persecution.[63] He pushed for the development of a native Chinese clergy, and supported the efforts of French missionaries to enter China, although he knew this would anger the Portuguese. He urged the development of an overland route from Europe to China through Russia. His tact was certainly greater than Schall's, his talents as multifaceted, and success seemed within his grasp. But at the peak of his accomplishments and prestige, in 1687 at the age of sixty-four, he was thrown from his horse and suffered serious internal injuries. He died the following year. K'ang-hsi ordered a state funeral and sacrifices to be offered in his name, and the Jesuit was taken to his final rest in splendid Chinese style. . . .

There seemed no reason why Verbiest's death need interrupt the steady pattern of missionary successes in China, and at first all went well for his successors. Rewards were heaped on the Jesuits who worked as mediators between China and Russia in drawing up the 1689 Treaty of Nerchinsk. An "edict of toleration" of the Christian religion was issued in 1692 after Jesuits had cured K'ang-hsi of a dangerous malarial fever by using quinine. The Jesuits were given land inside the Imperial city to build a church, and were commissioned by K'ang hsi to undertake a full cartographic survey of his empire. K'ang-hsi remained affable and generous to the missionaries, often singling them out for special notice when he toured the provinces. Jesuits were regularly appointed to direct the Bureau of Astronomy, and their place as technicians of influence within the regular bureaucracy seemed assured.[64]

All these hopeful signs proved illusory, however, and the problems that had once plagued Schall flared up again: factional fighting between missionaries became increasingly bitter, leading in 1705 to the despatch of a papal emissary who managed to split the Jesuits in China irreparably and to alienate the Emperor.[65] The hostility of influential Chinese officials increased, and persecution of Christians became common in the provinces. There was now no European with the influence (and no Chinese official with the inclination) to stop them. In the eighteenth century, K'ang-hsi's son and grandson condoned open persecution of Christians, and Christianity was declared heterodox, though missionaries continued to serve at court as astronomers, as the makers of fountains and curios, or as painters and builders.[66] Finally, in the 1770's, the maligned and discredited Jesuit order was abolished in Europe, and fresh waves of violent persecution in China sent the remaining missionaries into exile or hiding. The first calculated attempt to win over the Chinese through Western technical expertise had clearly failed.

Yet despite these setbacks, Westerners remained optimistic concerning the opportunities that China offered. Missionary accounts kept alive the image of the Chinese Emperor as a possible subject for Christian conversion, insisted that his mandarins were enlightened bureaucrats already on the path to truth, and described each act of persecution as a prelude to ever greater triumphs for the Faith. Theorists like Voltaire and Adam Smith used examples from China to reinforce their critiques of their own societies; others responded in a more light-hearted manner, embracing the gay extravagances of "Chinoiserie" which brought pagodas into British gardens, willowware to Western dinner tables, and Manchu pigtails to the heads of both King George III and George Washington.[67]

Western analysis of China was, in fact, inaccurate and sentimental. Confident of the superiority of their expertise and sure that China needed them, the first generations of Western advisers had simplified China to suit their purposes, had failed to understand the strength and impermeability of the Confucian moral structure, and had dismissed the hostility they often encountered as a temporary aberration.

Looking back from our own vantage point to the time of Schall and Verbiest, we can see that on balance it was the Chinese who had gained from the exchange. They had used the Westerners' skills when it suited them, and paid a fair price, but had offered little else in return. What did not concern them they had shrugged aside. By the early nineteenth-century Western religion was but a blurred memory. As the widely read scholar and eminent official Lin Tse-hsü put it in 1840: "It appears that the

Jesus-religion preached by Matteo Ricci was Catholicism, whereas the Jesus-religion preached afterwards by Verbiest was Christianity. The two terms 'Catholic' and 'Christian' must express some such difference."[68]

But the Westerners were not to dismiss the matter so lightly. The convergence symbolized by Schall's appointment had become an integral part of Western thinking. In China lay opportunity, and expertise was still the key. "It was a star that long ago led the Three Kings to adore the True God," Verbiest had written in 1674. "In the same way the science of the stars will lead the rulers of the Orient, little by little, to know and to adore their Lord."[69] Just because this particular forecast had proved overoptimistic, there was no need to abandon the strategy. There was no need to abandon it, indeed, even if one sought to bring the Chinese to other gods, through other sciences.

END NOTES

These notes give the citations for all material quoted in the text, and also the names of works that were of general relevance to each topic treated. Since few works were used for more than one chapter, there seemed no point in printing a separate bibliography. Accordingly, each book is fully listed under the note where it is first cited, and referred to thereafter by author's name and short title. In the rare cases in which a work was used in more than one chapter, the full listing has been repeated. A complete bibliography for each adviser, in other words, can be found in the notes to the chapter dealing with that adviser.

1. Adapted from Fu Lo-shu, *A Documentary Chronicle of Sino-Western Relations (1644–1820)*, 2 vols. (Tucson, University of Arizona Press, 1966), p. 3.
2. Adapted from ibid., p. 4.
3. For expansion of these points, cf. J. K. Fairbank and S. Y. Teng, "On the Ch'ing Tributary System," *Harvard Journal of Asiatic Studies*, 6 (1941), 135–246. Donald Lach, *Asia in the Making of Europe* (Chicago, University of Chicago Press, 1965). R. A. Skelton, *Explorers' Maps: Chapters in the Cartographic Record of Geographical Discovery* (New York, Praeger, 1958).
4. The major work on Matteo Ricci is Pasquale d'Elia, *Fonti ricciane; documenti originali concernenti Matteo Ricci e la storia della prime relazioni tra l'Europa e la Cina (1579–1615)*, 3 vols. (Rome, Libreria dello Stato, 1942–1949). For biographies of Jesuits in China, cf. Louis Pfister, S.J., *Notices biographiques et bibliographiques sur les Jésuites de l'ancienne mission de Chine, 1552–1773,* 2 vols. (Shanghai, Imprimerie de la Mission Catholique, 1932 and 1934). The best survey of early Jesuits in China is George H. Dunne, S.J., *Generation of Giants: The Story of the Jesuits in China in the Last Decades of the Ming Dynasty* (London, Burns and Oates, 1962). The best account of the Ch'ing missions is Arnold H. Rowbotham, *Missionary and Mandarin: The Jesuits at the Court of China* (Berkeley and Los Angeles, University of California Press, 1942).
5. For Mendoza's sources, cf. C. R. Boxer, *South China in the Sixteenth Century, Being*

the *Narratives of Galeote Pereira, Fr. Gaspar da Cruz, O.P., Fr. Martín de Rada, O.E.S.A. (1550–1575)* (London, Hakluyt Society, 1953).

6. Louis J. Gallagher, S.J., *China in the Sixteenth Century: The Journals of Matthew Ricci, 1583–1610* (New York, Random House, 1953), pp. 22–23

7. Gallagher, *Ricci Journals,* p. 154.

8. Dunne, *Jesuits,* pp. 210–211; Väth, *Schall,* pp. 40–41.

9. Dunne, *Jesuits,* pp. 130–145; Väth, *Schall,* pp. 41–46.

10. Väth, *Schall,* pp. 54–66.

11. *Lettres et mémoires d'Adam Schall S.J.,* ed. Henri Bernard, S.J. (relation historique, texte latin avec traduction française du P. Paul Bornet, S.J.) (Tientsin, Hautes Etudes, 1942), p. 4.

12. Arthur W. Hummel, ed., *Eminent Chinese of the Ch'ing Period (1644–1912),* 2 vols. (Washington, D.C., United States Government Printing Office, 1943), p. 453.

13. Franz Michael, *The Origin of Manchu Rule in China* (Baltimore, Johns Hopkins Press, 1942). Charles O. Hucker, *The Censorial System of Ming China* (Palo Alto, Stanford University Press, 1966).

14. Schall, *Memoirs,* p. 6.

15. Ibid., p. 10; and Pasquale M. d'Elia, S.J., *Galileo in China, Relations through the Roman College between Galileo and the Jesuit Scientist-Missionaries (1610–1640)* trans. Rufus Suter and Matthew Sciascia (Cambridg, Mass., Harvard University Press, 1960), p. 34.

16. Pfister, *Notices biographiques,* p. 163; Hummel, *Eminent Chinese,* pp. 807–809; Väth, *Schall,* pp. 74–75.

17. Hummel, *Eminent Chinese,* p. 317.

18. d'Elia, *Galileo,* pp. 27–32; Dunne, *Jesuits,* p. 214; Joseph Needham, *Science and Civilization in China* (Cambridge, Cambridge University Press, 1954), vol. 3, pp. 437–438; Henri Bernard, "L'encyclopédie astronomique du Père Schall," *Monumenta Serica,* 3 (1938), 35–77, 441–527.

19. Schall, *Memoirs,* pp. 14–16; Pfister, *Notices biographiques,* p. 180; Dunne, *Jesuits,* p. 309.

20. Schall, *Memoirs,* pp. 76, 92, 46.

21. Ibid., pp. 50–60.

22. Pfister, *Notices biographiques,* p. 165; Dunne, *Jesuits,* p. 312.

23. Schall, *Memoirs,* p. 84.

24. Ibid., pp. 86, 90, 102.

25. Ibid., p. 114.

26. Ibid., p. 132.

27. Ibid., p. 142.

28. Ibid., pp. 190, 216, 238; Fu Lo-shu, *Documentary Chronicle,* p. 4.

29. Schall, *Memoirs,* p. 192.

30. Ibid., p. 242.

31. Ibid., p. 362.

32. Ibid., pp. 210, 246–248; Pfister, *Notices biographiques,* pp. 170–171.

33. Schall, *Memoirs,* pp. 272–284.

34. Yuan Tschen, "Johann Adam Schall von Bell S.J. und der Bonzer Mu Tschen-wen," trans. D. W. Yang, *Monumenta Serica,* 5 (1940), 316–328.

35. Schall, *Memoirs,* p. 98.

36. John Nieuhoff, *An Embassy from the East-India Company of the United Provinces to the Grand Tartar Chain, Emperor of China,* trans. John Ogilby (London, John Macock, 1669), pp. 117–118.

37. Dunne, *Jesuits,* p. 333.
38. Ibid., pp. 325–328; Kenneth Scott Latourette, *A History of Christian Missions in China* (New York, Macmillan, 1929), pp. 131–138; François Bontinck, *La lutte autour de la liturgie chinoise aux XVII et XVIII siècles* (Louvain, Editions Nauwelaerts, 1962).
39. J. S. Cummins, ed., *The Travels and Controversies of Friar Domingo Navarrete, 1618–1686,* 2 vols. (Cambridge, Cambridge University Press, 1962), II, p. 190.
40. Anastasius van den Wyngaert, ed., *Relationes et Epistolas Fratrum Minorum Saeculi XVII, Sinica Franciscana* (Florence, 1936), III, p. 90; Dunne, *Jesuits,* p. 229.
41. Condensed from Fu Lo-shu, *Documentary Chronicle,* pp. 35–36.
42. Cummins, *Navarrete,* p. lxxvii.
43. Schall, *Memoirs,* p. 136.
44. Ibid., p. 302. Written before the final persecution, but typical of his views.
45. Ibid., p. 5. H. Bosmans, S.J., "Ferdinand Verbiest, directeur de l'observatoire de Peking (1623–1688)," *Revue des Questions Scientifiques,* 71 (1912), pp. 195–273 and 375–464; Quotation, pp. 203–204.
46. The biographical data is drawn from Bosmans, *Verbiest;* Pfister, *Notices biographiques,* pp. 338–362; Rowbotham, *Jesuits.*
47. Josson and Willaert, *Verbiest Correspondence,* p. 123.
48. Fu Lo-shu, *Documentary Chronicle,* p. 43.
49. Adapted from ibid., p. 44.
50. Bosmans, *Verbiest,* p. 256.
51. Needham, *Science in China,* vol. 3, pp. 451–452.
52. Bosmans, *Verbiest,* p. 265.
53. Ibid., p. 269.
54. Ibid., p. 383.
55. Ibid., pp. 385–387.
56. For a sceptic, cf. Matteo Ripa, *Memoirs of Father Ripa, During Thirteen Years' Residence at the Court of Peking in the Service of the Emperor of China,* trans. Fortunato Prandi (London, J. Murray, 1844).
57. Fu Lo-shu, *Documentary Chronicle,* p. 48.
58. Ibid., p. 58; Bosmans, *Verbiest,* p. 390.
59. J. B. du Halde, *Description géographique, historique, chronologique et physique de l'Empire de la Chine* (Paris, Le Mercier, 1735), IV, p. 75.
60. Ibid., p. 77.
61. Ibid., p. 80.
62. Fu Lo-shu, *Documentary Chronicle,* p. 69. Henri Bernard, "Ferdinand Verbiest, continuateur de l'oeuvre scientifique d'Adam Schall," *Monumenta Serica, 5* (1940), 103–140; cited activities on pp. 116–119.
63. *Sinica Franciscana,* III, p. 486; IV, p. 277; V, p. 115.
64. Joseph Sebes, S.J., *The Jesuits and the Sino-Russian Treaty of Nerchinsk (1689)* (Rome, Institutum Historicum S.I., 1961); Jonathan Spence, *Ts'ao Yin and the K'ang-hsi Emperor, Bond servant and Master* (New Haven, Yale University Press, 1966); Walter Fuchs, "Materialen zur Kartographie der Mandju-Zeit," *Monumenta Serica, 1* (1935), 386–427, and 3 (1937–38), 189–231.
65. Antonio Sisto Rosso, O.F.M., *Apostolic Legations to China of the Eighteenth Century* (South Pasadena, P. D. and Ione Perkins, 1948); Francis A. Rouleau, S.J., "Maillard de Tournon, Papal Legate at the Court of Peking," *Archivum Historicum Societatis Iesu, 31* (1962), 264–323.
66. Bernward H. Willeke, O.F.M., *Imperial Government and Catholic Missions in China During the Years 1784–1785* (St. Bonaventure, New York, The Franciscan Institute,

1948); J. J. M. de Groot, *Sectarianism and Religious Persecution in China,* 2 vols, (Leiden, E. J. Brill, 1901); Ishida Mikinosuke, "A Biographical Study of Giuseppe Castiglione (Lang Shih-ning), a Jesuit Painter in the Court of Peking under the Ch'ing Dynasty," *Memoirs of the Research Department of the Toyo Bunko, 19* (1960), 79–121.

67. G. F. Hudson, *Europe and China, A Survey of their Relations from the Earliest Times to 1800* (Boston, Beacon, 1961); Adolf Reichwein, *China and Europe; Intellectual and Artistic Contacts in the Eighteenth Century* (New York, Knopf, 1925); *Lettres édifiantes et curieuses concernant l'Asie, L'Afrique et l'Amérique* (Paris, various eds., 1713–1843); Basil Guy, *The French Image of China Before and After Voltaire* (Geneva, 1963).

68. Arthur Waley, *The Opium War Through Chinese Eyes* (New York, Macmillan, 1958), p. 97.

69. Bosmans, *Verbiest,* p. 386.

QUESTIONS

1. How were the Jesuits able to gain high office in the Chinese government, bypassing the rigorous civil service examination system?

2. Why was astronomy so important to the Qing court? To the missionaries?

3. What were the most significant obstacles the Jesuits had to overcome to make an impact on the Chinese in the religious arena?

4. How successful was the Jesuit mission to China? Which proved the more powerful force in this East/West encounter and why?

The Slave Trade

DOCUMENT

A VENETIAN DESCRIBES THE PORTUGUESE WEST AFRICAN TRADE

Alvise da Cadamosto

Prince Henry the Navigator (1394–1460), fifth son of King John I of Portugal, was Europe's greatest patron of naval exploration and the most important precursor of Ferdinand and Isabella of Spain, who sponsored the voyages of Christopher Columbus. From his residence on the Sagres peninsula near Cape St. Vincent, Prince Henry organized a series of voyages that explored the islands of the Atlantic and the coast of Africa as far south as Sierra Leone. Between 1420 and 1460 the Azores, the Canary Islands, and Madeira were discovered and settled by Portuguese fishermen and sailors. Prince Henry replaced the casual fishing and trading voyages typical of the early fifteenth century with a systematic program of progressive exploration much further south. He has sometimes been described as a Renaissance humanistic prince, seeking to exploit the knowledge of the ancients and modern sciences to increase his power, but there is little to support this interpretation, and modern historians tend to place his mental outlook firmly within that of the late-Medieval world.

The selection given here is from an account of the Portuguese West African trade by Alvise da Ca'da Mosto or Cadamosto (c. 1426–1483), a Venetian merchant who was licensed by Prince Henry to trade in Guinea. He made two voyages, probably in 1455–56, as commander of a Portuguese expedition

Reprinted from *The Voyages of Cadamosto*, translated by G.R. Crone, by permission of David Higham Associates. Copyright © 1937 by the Hakluyt Society.

down the coast of Africa, and is credited with the discovery of Cape Verde. His account of his expeditions, published posthumously in 1507, describes the native populations and discusses how Africans responded to their encounters with Europeans. His account is strictly that of a businessman, and lacks the fantastical details usually found in late-Medieval travel literature.

THE VOYAGES OF CADAMOSTA

Chapter IX
The Description of Capo Bianco and the Islands Nearest to It

We set sail from this island[1] making due south towards Ethiopia; and in a few days reached Capo Blanco about 770 miles from the Canaries. It is to be noted that, leaving these islands to sail towards this cape, one goes along the coast of Africa which is constantly on the left hand; you sail well offshore, however, and do not sight land, because the Isole di Canaria are very far out to sea to the west, each one further than its neighbour. Thus you keep a course far out from land, until you have covered at least two-thirds of the passage from the islands to Capo Bianco and then draw near on the left hand to the coast until land is sighted, in order not to run past the said Cape without recognising it, because beyond it no land is seen for a considerable distance. The coast runs back at this cape, forming a gulf which is called the "Forna dargin."[2] This name Dargin is derived from an islet in the gulf called Argin by the people of the country. This gulf runs in more than fifty miles, and there are three more islands, to which the Portuguese have given these names: Isola Bianca, from its sands: Isola da le Garze,[3] because the first Portuguese found on it so many eggs of these sea birds that they loaded two boats from the caravels with them: the third Isola de Cuori. All are small, sandy, and uninhabited. On this Dargin there is a supply of fresh water, but not on the others.

Note that when you set out beyond the Strecto de Zibelterra [keeping this coast on the left hand, that is, of Barbary] towards Ethiopia, you do not find it inhabited by these Barbari except as far as the Cauo de Chantin.[4] From this cape along the coast to Capo Blanco commences the sandy country which is the desert that ranges on its northern confines with the mountains, which cut off our Barbary from Tunis, and from all these

60

places of the coast. This desert the Berbers call Sarra:[5] on the south it marches with the Blacks of lower Ethiopia: it is a very great desert, which takes well-mounted men fifty to sixty days to cross—in some places more, and some less. The boundary of this desert is on the Ocean Sea at the coast, which is everywhere sandy, white, arid, and all equally low-lying: it does not appear to be higher in one place than another, as far as the said Capo Bianco, which is so called because the Portuguese who discovered it saw it to be sandy and white, without signs of grass or trees whatsoever. It is a very fine cape, like a triangle, that is, on its face; it has three points, distant the one from the other about a mile.

On this coast there are very large fisheries[6] of various and most excellent large fish without number, like those of our Venetian fisheries, and other kinds. Throughout this Forna Dargin there is little water, and there are many shoals, some of sand, others of rock. There are strong currents in the sea, on account of which one navigates only by day, with the lead in hand, and according to the state of the tide. Two ships have already been wrecked upon these banks. The aforesaid Cauo de Chantin stands approximately north-east of Capo Bianco.

You should also know that behind this Cauo Bianco on the land, is a place called Hoden,[7] which is about six days inland by camel. This place is not walled, but is frequented by Arabs, and is a market where the caravans arrive from Tanbutu,[8] and from other places in the land of the Blacks, on their way to our nearer Barbary. The food of the peoples of this place is dates, and barley, of which there is sufficient, for they grow in some of these places, but not abundantly. They drink the milk of camels and other animals, for they have no wine. They also have cows and goats, but not many, for the land is dry. Their oxen and cows, compared with ours, are small.

They are Muhammadans, and very hostile to Christians. They never remain settled, but are always wandering over these deserts. These are the men who go to the land of the Blacks, and also to our nearer Barbary. They are very numerous, and have many camels on which they carry brass and silver from Barbary and other things to Tanbuto and to the land of the Blacks. Thence they carry away gold and pepper,[9] which they bring hither. They are brown complexioned, and wear white cloaks edged with a red stripe: their women also dress thus, without shifts. On their heads the men

61

wear turbans in the Moorish fashion, and they always go barefooted. In these sandy districts there are many lions, leopards, and ostriches, the eggs of which I have often eaten and found good.

You should know that the said Lord Infante of Portugal has leased this island of Argin to Christians [for ten years], so that no one can enter the bay to trade with the Arabs save those who hold the license. These have dwellings on the island and factories where they buy and sell with the said Arabs who come to the coast to trade for merchandise of various kinds, such as woollen cloths, cotton, silver, and "alchezeli,"[10] that is, cloaks, carpets, and similar articles and above all, corn, for they are always short of food. They give in exchange slaves whom the Arabs bring from the land of the Blacks,[11] and gold *tiber*.[12] The Lord Infante therefore caused a castle[13] to be built on the island to protect this trade for ever. For this reason, Portuguese caravels are coming and going all the year to this island.

These Arabs also have many Berber horses,[14] which they trade, and take to the Land of the Blacks, exchanging them with the rulers for slaves. Ten or fifteen slaves are given for one of these horses, according to their quality. The Arabs likewise take articles of Moorish silk, made in Granata and in Tunis of Barbary, silver, and other goods, obtaining in exchange any number of these slaves, and some gold. These slaves are brought to the market and town of Hoden; there they are divided: some go to the mountains of Barcha,[15] and thence to Sicily, [others to the said town of Tunis and to all the coasts of Barbary], and others again are taken to this place, Argin, and sold to the Portuguese leaseholders. As a result every year the Portuguese carry away from Argin a thousand slaves.[16] Note that before this traffic was organized, the Portuguese caravels, sometimes four, sometimes more, were wont to come armed to the Golfo d'Argin, and descending on the land by night, would assail the fisher villages, and so ravage the land. Thus they took of these Arabs both men and women, and carried them to Portugal for sale: behaving in a like manner along all the rest of the coast, which stretches from Cauo Bianco to the Rio di Senega and even beyond. This is a great river, dividing a race which is called Azanaghi[17] from the first Kingdom of the Blacks. These Azanaghi are brownish, rather dark brown than light, and live in places along this coast beyond Cauo Bianco, and many of them are spread over this desert inland. They are neighbours of the above mentioned Arabs of Hoden.

They live on dates, barley, and camel's milk: but as they are very near the first land of the Blacks, they trade with them, obtaining from this land of the Blacks millet and certain vegetables, such as beans, upon which they support themselves. They are men who require little food and can withstand hunger, so that they sustain themselves throughout the day upon a mess of barley porridge. They are obliged to do this because of the want of victuals they experience. These, as I have said, are taken by the Portuguese as before mentioned and are the best slaves of all the Blacks. But, however, for some time all have been at peace and engaged in trade. The said Lord Infante will not permit further hurt to be done to any, because he hopes that, mixing with Christians, they may without difficulty be converted to our faith, not yet being firmly attached to the tenets of Muhammad, save from what they know by hearsay.

These same Azanaghi have a strange custom: they always wear a hand-kerchief on the head with a flap[18] which they bring across the face, covering the mouth and part of the nose. For they say that the mouth is a brutish thing, that is always uttering wind and bad odours so that it should be kept covered, and not displayed, likening it almost to the posterior, and that these two portions should be kept covered. It is true that they never uncover it, except when they eat, and not otherwise for I have seen many of them.

There are no lords among them, save those who are richer: these are honoured and obeyed to some degree by the others. They are a very poor people, liars, the biggest thieves in the world, and exceedingly treacherous. They are men of average height, and spare. They wear their hair in locks down to their shoulders, almost in the German fashion—but their hair is black, and anointed every day with fish oil, so that it smells strongly, the which they consider a great refinement.

Chapter XI[19]
The Exchange of Salt for Gold: and the Distance It Travels

That woman who has the largest breasts is considered more beautiful than the others: with the result that each woman, to increase their size, at the age of seventeen or eighteen when the breasts are already formed, places across her chest a cord, which she binds around the breasts, and draws tight with much force; in this way the breasts are distended, and frequent pulling every day causes them to grow and lengthen so much that many reach the navel. Those that have the biggest prize them as a rare thing.

You should know that these people have no knowledge of any Christians except the Portuguese, against whom they have waged war for [thirteen or] fourteen years, many of them having been taken prisoners, as I have already said, and sold into slavery. It is asserted that when for the first time they saw sails, that is, ships, on the sea (which neither they nor their forefathers had ever seen before), they believed that they were great sea-birds with white wings, which were flying, and had come from some strange place: when the sails were lowered for the landing, some of them, watching from far off, thought that the ships were fishes. Others again said that they were phantoms that went by night, at which they were greatly terrified. The reason for this belief was because these caravels within a short space of time appeared at many places, where attacks were delivered, especially at night, by their crews. Thus one such assault might be separated from the next by a hundred or more miles, according to the plans of the sailors, or as the winds, blowing hither and thither, served them. Perceiving this, they said amongst themselves, "If these be human creatures, how can they travel so great a distance in one night, a distance which we could not go in three days?" Thus, as they did not understand the art of navigation, they all thought that the ships were phantoms. This I know is testified to by many Portuguese who at that time were trading in caravels on this coast, and also by those who were captured on these raids. And from this it may be judged how strange many of our ways appeared to them, if such an opinion could prevail.

Beyond the said mart of Edon [Oden], six days journey further inland, there is a place called Tagaza, that is to say in our tongue "cargador,"[20] where a very great quantity of rock-salt is mined. Every year large caravans of camels belonging to the above mentioned Arabs and Azanaghi, leaving in many parties, carry it to Tanbutu,[21] thence they go to Melli,[22] the empire of the Blacks, where, so rapidly is it sold, within eight days of its arrival all is disposed of at a price of two to three hundred *mitigalli*[23] a load, according to the quantity: [a *mitigallo* is worth about a ducat:] then with the gold they return to their homes.

In this empire of Melli it is very hot, and the pasturage is very unsuitable for four footed animals: so that of the majority which come with the caravans no more than twenty-five out of a hundred return. There are no quadrupeds in this country, because they all die, and many also of the Arabs and Azanaghi sicken in this place and die, on account of the great heat. It is said that on horseback it is about forty days from Tagaza to Tanbutu, and thirty from Tanbutu to Melli.

I enquired of them what the merchants of Melli did with this salt, and was told that a small quantity is consumed in their country. Since it is below the meridional and on the equinoctial, where the day is constantly about as long as the night, it is extremely hot at certain seasons of the year: this causes the blood to putrefy, so that were it not for this salt, they would die. The remedy they employ is as follows: they take a small piece of the salt, mix it in a jar with a little water, and drink it every day. They say that this saves them. The remainder of this salt they carry away on a long journey in pieces as large as a man can, with a certain knack, bear on his head.

You must know that when this salt is carried to Melli by camel it goes in large pieces [as it is dug out from the mines], of a size most easily carried on camels, two pieces on each animal. Then at Melli, these blacks break it in smaller pieces, in order to carry it on their heads, so that each man carries one piece, and thus they form a great army of men on foot, who transport it a great distance. Those who carry it have two forked sticks, one in each hand: when they are tired, they plant them in the ground, and rest their load upon them. In this way they carry it until they reach certain waters: I could not learn from them whether it is fresh or sea water, so that I do not know if it is a river or the sea, though they consider it to be the sea. [I think however it must be a river, for if it were the sea, in such a hot country there would be no lack of salt.] These Blacks are obliged to carry it in this way, because they have no camels or other beasts of burden, as these cannot live in the great heat. It may be imagined how many men are required to carry it on foot, and how many are those who consume it every year. Having reached these waters with the salt, they proceed in this fashion: all those who have the salt pile it in rows, each marking his own. Having made these piles, the whole caravan retires half a day's journey. Then there come another race of blacks who do not wish to be seen or to speak. They arrive in large boats, from which it appears that they come from islands, and disembark. Seeing the salt, they place a quantity of gold opposite each pile, and then turn back, leaving salt and gold.

65

When they have gone, the negroes who own the salt return: if they are satisfied with the quantity of gold, they leave the salt and retire with the gold. Then the blacks of the gold return, and remove those piles which are without gold. By other piles of salt they place more gold, if it pleases them, or else they leave the salt. In this way, by long and ancient custom, they carry on their trade without seeing or speaking to each other. Although it is difficult to believe this, I can testify that I have had this information from many merchants, Arab as well as Azanaghi, and also from persons in whom faith can be placed.

Chapter XIV
The Rio de Senega, Which Divides the Desert from the Fertile Land

When we had passed in sight of this Cauo Bianco, we sailed on our journey to the river called the Rio de Senega, the first river of the Land of the Blacks, which debouches on this coast. This river separates the Blacks from the brown people called Azanaghi, and also the dry and arid land, that is, the above mentioned desert, from the fertile country of the Blacks. The river is large; its mouth being over a mile wide, and quite deep. There is another mouth a little distance beyond, with an island between. Thus it enters the sea by two mouths, and before each of them about a mile out to sea are shoals and broad sand-banks. In this place the water increases and decreases every six hours, that is, with the rise and fall of the tide. The tide ascends the river more than sixty miles, according to the information I have had from Portuguese who have been [many miles] up it [in caravels]. He who wishes to enter this river must go in with the tide, on account of the shoals and banks at the mouth. From Cauo Bianco it is 380 miles to the river: all the coast is sandy within about twenty miles of the mouth. It is called Costa de Antte rotte, and is of the Azanaghi, or brown men.

It appears to me a very marvellous thing that beyond the river all men are very black, tall and big, their bodies well formed; and the whole country green, full of trees, and fertile: while on this side, the men are brownish, small, lean, ill-nourished, and small in stature: the country sterile and arid. This river is said to be a branch of the river Nile, of the four royal rivers: it flows through all Ethiopia, watering the country as in Egypt: passing through "lo caiero," it waters all the land of Egypt.

66

Chapter XXXIX
The Elevation of Our North Star; and the Six Stars Opposite

During the days we spent at the mouth of this river,[24] we saw the pole star once only; it appeared very low down over the sea, therefore we could see it only when the weather was very clear. It appeared about a third of a lance above the horizon. We also had sight of six stars low down over the sea, clear, bright, and large. By the compass, they stood due south, in the following fashion.[25]

This we took to be the southern wain, though we did not see the principal star, for it would not have been possible to sight it unless we had lost the north star. In this place we found the night to be 13 [eleven and a half] hours, and the day 11 [twelve and a half] hours, that is, in the first days of July, or more accurately on the second of the month.

This country is hot at all seasons of the year. It is true that there is some variation, and what they call a winter: thus beginning in the afore-said month [of July] until the end of October it rains continuously almost every day from noon, in the following way: clouds rise continually over the land from the E.N.E., or from the E.S.E., with very heavy thunder, lightning and thunderbolts. Thus an excessive quantity of rain falls, and at this season the negroes begin to sow in the same manner as those of the kingdom of Senega. Their sustenance is entirely millet and vegetables, flesh and milk.

I understand that in the interior of this country, [on account of the great heat of the air] the rain which falls is warm. In the morning, when day breaks, there is no dawn at the rising of the sun, as in our parts, where between dawn and sunrise there is a short interval before the shadows of night disperse: the sun appears suddenly, though it is not light for the space of half an hour, as the sun is dull and, as it were, smoky on first rising. The cause of this appearance of the sun early in the morning, contrary to what happens in our country, cannot, I think, arise from any other circumstance than the extreme lowness of the land, devoid of mountains, and all my companions were of this opinion.

END NOTES

1. Palma. The distance is about 570 nautical miles.
2. Arguim, discovered in 1443 by Nuno Tristão, where a fort was erected by Prince Henry in 1448 for the protection of merchants. Its good water and safe anchorage quickly made it a valuable *entrepôt*, and it became an important trading centre. The Arab name was "Ghir," and Azurara calls it "Gete."
3. Island of Herons (Azurara: I, p. 63, and II, pp. 320–1), one of the Arguim Islands. The big expedition of 1444 rested here and refreshed themselves on the multitude of young birds.
4. Cape Cantin, 32° 36' N., 9° 14' W.
5. Sahara. The mountains are the Atlas range.
6. The fishing fields were already being exploited under Prince Henry's license.
7. Wadan, an important desert market about 350 miles east of Arguim. Later, in 1487, when the Portuguese were endeavouring to penetrate the interior they attempted to establish a trading factory at Wadan which acted as a feeder to Arguim, tapping the north-bound caravan traffic and diverting some of it to the west coast.
8. Timbuktu
9. Malaguetta pepper
10. Probably the coarse cloth called by El Bekri in the eleventh century "chigguiza," which was doubtless the "shigge" purchased by Barth in Timbuktu in the nineteenth century (Barth: *Travels,* iv, p. 443).
11. The Portuguese had now established in West Africa the insidious practice of inciting the coast tribes to raid their neighbours for slaves.
12. The Arabic *thibr* or *tibar,* meaning gold dust.
13. Built by Prince Henry in 1448.
14. Leo Africanus, writing in the sixteenth century, makes several references to the trade in Barbary horses for which there was an excellent market in the Sudan. Later the Portuguese regularly shipped out horses to barter for slaves.
15. Barca in Cyrenaica
16. According to Azurara (II, p. 288), up to the year 1448 the total number of Africans who had been carried captive to Portugal during Prince Henry's time was only 927. This passage indicates how rapidly the slave trade was increasing.
17. The Azanaghi or Azaneguys, as Azurara calls them, were the Sanhaja, historically the most important of the Tuareg tribes, and widely distributed over the western Sahara.
18. The *litham,* still worn by the Tuareg; hence their name Muleththemin, meaning the Veiled People. In Roman and Byzantine times they appear not to have worn the veil, and when or why they took to it remains a problem to which no acceptable solution has been found. Its use appears always to have been restricted to the men.
19. This and subsequent chapters are misnumbered in the original version.
20. "A load, or charge"; other texts have "bisaccia d'oro", i.e. wallet of gold, the gold not being obtained locally, but in exchange for salt.
21. Timbuktu
22. Mali
23. One *mithgal* or *mitkal* equalled about ⅛ oz. of gold.
24. The Gambia
25. The first recorded notice of the Southern Cross.

QUESTIONS

1. What features does Cadamosto focus on as he describes the islands and waters along the African coast? Why does he concentrate on these features?

2. What commodities are traded between the Arabs and the Portuguese? Where do the Arabs get the goods they exchange with the Portuguese?

3. Who are the Azanaghi? How does Cadamosto describe them and why does he want to provide so much detail about them?

4. How is salt used? How is the salt trade conducted?

SLAVE TRADE IN THE KINGDOM OF LOANGO IN THE EIGHTEENTH CENTURY

Abbé Proyart

Abbé Proyart's Histoire de Loango, Kakongo et autres royaumes d'Afrique *was published in 1776 and quickly became a seminal text on the geography and economy of Central Africa. The regions of Loango and Kakongo are in the region of present-day Congo and Angola. The precision and detail of the account indicate that it relies on firsthand observation, but it is unclear whether it is based on Proyart's own experiences or on those of other travelers.*

The main trade of these people is in slaves whom they sell to the Europeans, that is to say, to the French, English and Dutch who then ship them to their colonies in America. Slaves originating from Loango and the neighbouring kingdoms are considered as the darkest and the strongest in Africa. They have been captured in battle by those who sell them.

Those who captured them either sell them to native merchants or take them to the coast, but they are absolutely forbidden to sell them directly to the Europeans. They must go through brokers, appointed by the Minister of Commerce, who deal with ship captains. These slaves are valued according to their age, sex and physical strength. Goods from Europe are used in payment.

Although the different Kingdoms about which we are talking are quite close to one another, the manner of evaluating goods as against slaves is not the same. On the coasts of Malimbe and Cabinde, that is to say the Kingdoms of Kakongo and n'Goio, the calculation is done in *wares,* and in Loango it is in *pieces.* A *ware* is a piece of calico or Indian linen measuring 12 to 16 metres. Before selling, the blacks go to the warehouse of the captain, which is on the sea shore, to indicate the pieces of material that they will accept. A man who sold four slaves at fifteen *wares* per head, will receive sixty pieces of a designated material. In Kingdoms where buying is done in *wares,* it is usual to give, for each slave, what is known as *bonus,* which normally consists of three or four bottles of brandy, fifteen pounds of gun powder and some dozens of Knives. Other goods can be given in place of those mentioned.

In Loango the calculation is done in *pieces.* Here all sorts of goods are put together with linen materials to form a *piece.* Thus, when a slave is said to cost thirty pieces, it does not mean that he is worth thirty pieces of linen fabric, but rather thirty times an ideal value considered adequate to be called *piece,* such that a single piece of linen fabric is sometimes estimated at two or three *pieces,* just as several objects are sometimes required to make one piece. This difference in ways of counting is of little import in the final analysis as the price of slaves is roughly the same in all neighbouring Kingdoms of

A scrutiny of the account that follows will help us to estimate the real value of the *piece* and to see what goods are commonly passed on to blacks in exchange for their slaves.

I paid to Ma-nboukou, for the slave Makouta, aged twenty-two years, whom he sold to me for thirty pieces:

One Indian linen material 16 metres long,
valued at two ad half pieces.. .. ..   2 1/2p
Two guineas (dark blue calico) valued at
two and a half pieces each   5
One chasselat and one bajuta skin measuring
16 metres each (calico materials) valued at four pieces   4
One neganoskin 16 metres long and one 12 metres
long, "nicané" (other calico materials) valued at
three and a half pieces 3 1/2

One piece of cambric of 11 metres, valued at 1 1/2 pieces	1 1/2
One belt made of red cloth (1.2 metres long and one foot wide) valued at one piece	1
One rod (approximately two metres thick linen fabric) valued at one piece	1
Two standard guns, valued at two pieces	2
Two barrels of gun powder (approximately 5 pounds each), valued at two pieces	2
Two bags of bullets (weighing three pounds each) valued at half piece	1/2
Two sabres at a quarter piece each	1/2
Two dozens of standard knives with sheaths valued at half piece	1/2
Two iron bars weighing both 20 lbs valued at one piece	1
Five earthenware pots valued at half piece	1/2
Four barrels of brandy (each containing five bottles) valued at four pieces	4
Ten lines of glass stones (for making chaplets) valued at half piece	1/2
Total	30 pieces
In addition, I paid to the broker for his services, the value of six pieces in guns, gun powder, sabres and brandy	6
Grand Total	36 pieces

Apart from the agreed price for each slave, it is still necessary for the captain, at the conclusion of his business, to present gifts to the Minister of Commerce and to those brokers who have been of service to him and to whom he may have become attached. Such presents are in corals, silverware, rugs and other more or less precious commodities.

At the moment slaves are much more expensive that they were in the past, at least for French people; for it is possible for them to be relatively more expensive for one nation than for another. The French, the English and the Dutch all do their exchange with goods but these goods are different. Thus the expensiveness of slaves for a nation depends on the price that this nation puts on the goods she sends to the blacks; and again this price, as one would imagine, varies more or less with the level of understanding existing between the individuals engaged in the same trade.

The function of brokers is not limited to enhancing the trade in slaves; they are also responsible for ensuring that regulations made by the king or the Minister of commerce are implemented. The most slaves bought from outside the country can be sold as slaves to Europeans. Every slave born in the Kingdom is under the protection of the Commerce Minister and can invoke this protection against his master who may wish to sell him to the Europeans, unless he has given his master cause, through misconduct, to so sell him. For the law permits the master to dispose of a slave, no matter who he is, who is found guilty of infidelity, of rebellion or of any other criminal act. In order to prevent the violent and fraudulent practices that could characterize such a trade, the Commerce Minister of Kakongo forbade all brokers to carry out slave deals during the night. In addition, they are not allowed to send slaves to the European warehouses under the pretext of letting the captain have a preview. They are also forbidden to receive advance payments on slaves that they have not delivered without obtaining permission.

The slave trade is the only business that the French are doing on these coasts: trading in ivory, monkeys, parrots and some other such commodities is so negligible that it can be considered as non-existent. The English carry away, every year, from the forest of lomba, several shiploads of a particular red wood which is very good for dyeing, although inferior to that obtained from Brazil.

As has already been mentioned, the commerce that takes place on the coasts with foreigners involves only a small number of individuals, whom one can consider as the rich and powerful in the country. As for the masses, having no other needs but to feed and clothe themselves, in the most vulgar and simple manner, trading for them is limited to a few commodities. There is daily market in the towns and large villages; it takes place at the public square, under some big trees. Smoked fish, cassava and other tubers, salt, coconuts, sugar cane, bananas, plantains and some other fruits are sold there. It is on feast days that one notices greater crowds of sellers and buyers in these markets. There is no cheating in these markets.

A mother can send a child of six years to the markets, assured that no one will cheat the child. One does not have to understand the native language to buy from these markets: prices are never haggled. All commodities are divided into small equal portions, of the prescribed weight, and each portion is worth one macoute. There is no risk of a buyer being cheated in quality or quantity of what he is buying: the salt and cassava being displayed by one seller are just like the salt and cassava displayed by the other seller. Thus, without taking the trouble of comparing the commodities of one merchant with another's, you take, from the first person you meet, as many little packets as the macoutes you have can buy, and you give way to others.

QUESTIONS

1. How are the calculations of prices undertaken in Kakongo and Loango?
2. What is the role of brokers in the slave trade?
3. According to Proyart's account, how do Africans and Europeans each seek to direct the trade in slaves? Which side seems to be most successful in exerting control?
4. What does Proyart's list of goods traded for a slave suggest about life in eighteenth-century Central Africa?

from CHAPTER 3, "THE SLAVESHIP" *in* EQUIANO'S TRAVELS

Olaudah Equiano

Olaudah Equiano was born around 1745 in what is now Nigeria. Equiano was kidnapped and enslaved at about the age of ten. After a period of bondage in Africa, Equiano was transported to the West Indies, and from there to Virginia, where he was sold to a planter. Resold to an officer in the British navy, Equiano—renamed Gustavo Vassa by his new master—witnessed the hostilities of the Seven Years War aboard a Royal Navy ship. In 1762, the naval officer reneged on an earlier promise to free Equiano, and instead sold him in the West Indies. Equiano was able to purchase his own freedom in 1766, using funds he had earned through personal enterprise. As a freedman, Equiano was involved in several commercial voyages, sailing as far as the North Pole before he settled in London. There, Equiano converted to Methodism and emerged as an outspoken opponent of the slave trade. He married Susanna Cullen, an Englishwoman, in 1792, and left a sizable estate to their daughter when he died in 1797.

The Interesting Narrative was published in 1789. It was one of a series of works by authors of African birth or descent to appear before the public during this period. Writings by James Albert Ukawsaw Gronniosaw, Phillis Wheatley, and Ignatius Sancho were also published in Britain in the 1770s and 1780s. Like these publications, Equiano's work offered convincing evidence of the intellectual capability of Africans. But as the first Afro-Briton account to offer an indictment

Reprinted from *The Interesting Narrative and Other Writings*, 1789.

of the slave trade, the Interesting Narrative *was unique. It was praised by Mary Wollstonecraft and John Wesley, and ran through nine English language editions during Equiano's lifetime.* Equiano's Interesting Narrative *also reminds us of the mobility and mixing of cultures that characterized the Atlantic world in the eighteenth century. In this passage, Equiano described how he was transported aboard a slave ship to the Americas.*

The first object which saluted my eyes when I arrived on the coast was the sea, and a slave-ship, which was then riding at anchor, and waiting for its cargo. These filled me with astonishment, which was soon converted into terror, which I am yet at a loss to describe, nor the then feelings of my mind. When I was carried on board I was immediately handled, and tossed up, to see if I were sound,[1] by some of the crew; and I was now persuaded that I had gotten into a world of bad spirits, and that they were going to kill me.[2] Their complexions too differing so much from ours, their long hair, and the language they spoke, which was very different from any I had ever heard, united to confirm me in this belief. Indeed, such were the horrors of my views and fears at the moment, that, if ten thousand worlds had been my own, I would have freely parted with them all to have exchanged my condition with that of the meanest slave in my own country. When I looked round the ship too, and saw a large furnace of copper boiling, and a multitude of black people of every description chained together, every one of their countenances expressing dejection and sorrow, I no longer doubted of my fate, and, quite overpowered with horror and anguish, I fell motionless on the deck and fainted. When I recovered a little, I found some black people about me who I believed were some of those who brought me on board and had been receiving their pay; they talked to me in order to cheer me, but all in vain. I asked them if we were not to be eaten by those white men with horrible looks, red faces, and long hair.[3] They told me I was not; and one of the crew brought me a small portion of spirituous liquor in a wine glass; but, being afraid of him, I would not take it out of his hand. One of the blacks therefore took it from him and gave it to me, and I took a little down my palate, which, instead of reviving me, as they thought it would, threw me into the greatest consternation at the strange feeling it produced, having never tasted any such liquor before. Soon after this, the blacks who brought me on board went off, and left me abandoned to despair. I now saw myself deprived of all chance of returning to my native country, or even the least glimpse of hope of gaining the shore, which I now considered as friendly: and I even wished for my former slavery in preference to my present situation, which was filled with horrors of every kind, still heightened by my ignorance of what I was to undergo. I was not long suffered to indulge my grief; I was soon put down under the decks, and there I received such a salutation in my nostrils as I had never experienced in my life; so that with the loathsomeness of the stench, and crying together, I became so sick and low that I was not able to eat, nor had I the least desire to taste any thing. I now wished for the last friend, Death, to relieve me; but soon, to my grief, two of the white men offered me eatables; and, on my refusing to eat, one of them held me fast by the hands, and laid me across, I think, the windlass[4] and tied my feet, while the other flogged me severely. I had never experienced any thing of this kind before; and although, not being used to the water, I naturally feared that element the first time I saw it; yet, nevertheless, could I have got over the nettings,[5] I would have jumped over the side, but I could not; and, besides, the crew used to watch us very closely who were not chained down to the decks, lest we should leap into the water; and I have seen some of these poor African prisoners most severely cut for attempting to do so, and hourly whipped for not eating. This indeed was often the case with myself. In a little time after, amongst the poor chained men, I found some of my own nation, which in a small degree gave ease to my mind. I inquired of these what was to be done with us? they gave me to understand we were to be carried to these white people's country to work for them. I then was a little revived, and thought, if it were no worse than working, my situation was not so desperate: but still I feared I should be put to death, the white people looked and acted, as I thought, in so savage a manner; for I had never seen among any people such instances of brutal cruelty; and this not only shewn towards us blacks, but also to some of the whites themselves.[6] One white man in particular I saw, when we were permitted to be on deck, flogged so unmercifully with a large rope near the foremast,[7] that he died in consequence of it; and they tossed him over the side as they would have done a brute. This made me fear these people the more; and I expected nothing less than to be treated in the same manner. I could not help expressing my fears and apprehensions to some of my countrymen: I asked them if these people had no country, but lived in this hollow place the ship? they told me they did not, but came from a distant one. "Then," said I, "how comes it in all our country we never heard of them?" They told me, because they lived so very far off. I then asked where were their women? had they any like themselves! I was told they had: "And why," said I, "do we not see them?" they answered, because they were left behind. I asked how the vessel could go? they told me they could not tell; but that there were cloths put upon the masts by the help of the ropes I saw, and then the vessel went on; and the white men had some spell or magic they put in the water when they liked in order to stop the vessel.[8] I was exceedingly amazed at this account, and really thought they were spirits. I therefore wished much to be from amongst them, for I expected they would sacrifice me: but my wishes were vain; for we were so quartered that it was impossible for any of us to make our escape. While we staid on the coast I was mostly on deck; and one day, to my great astonishment, I saw one of these vessels coming in with the sails up. As soon as the whites saw it, they gave a great shout, at which we were amazed; and the more so as the vessel appeared larger by approaching nearer. At last she came to an anchor in my sight, and when the anchor was let go, I and my countrymen who saw it were lost in astonishment to observe the vessel stop; and were now convinced it was done by magic. Soon after this the other ship got her boats[9] out, and they came on board of us, and the people of both ships seemed very glad to see each other. Several of the strangers also shook hands with us black people, and made motions with their hands, signifying, I suppose, we were to go to their country; but we did not understand them. At last, when the ship we were in had got in all her cargo, they made ready with many fearful noises, and we were all put under deck, so that we could not see how they managed the vessel. But this disappointment was the least of my sorrow. The stench of the hold while we were on the coast was so intolerably loathsome, that it was dangerous to remain there for any time, and some of us had been permitted to stay on the deck for the fresh air; but now that the whole ship's cargo were confined together, it became absolutely pestilential. The closeness of the place, and the heat of the climate, added to the number in the ship, which was so crowded that each had scarcely room to turn himself, almost suffocated us. This produced copious perspirations, so that the air soon became unfit for respiration, from a variety of loathsome smells, and brought on a sickness among the slaves, of which many died, thus falling victims to the improvident avarice, as I may call it, of their purchasers. This wretched situation was again aggravated by the galling of the chains, now become insupportable; and the filth of the necessary tubs, into which the children often fell, and were almost suffocated.[10] The shrieks of the women, and the groans of the dying, rendered the whole a scene of horror almost inconceiveable. Happily perhaps for myself I was soon reduced so low here that it was thought necessary to keep me almost always on deck; and from my extreme youth I was not put in fetters. In this situation I expected every hour to share the fate of my companions, some of whom were almost daily brought upon deck at the point of death, which I began to hope would soon put an end to my miseries. Often did I think many of the inhabitants of the deep much more happy than myself; I envied them the freedom they enjoyed, and as often wished I could change my condition for theirs. Every circumstance I met with served only to render my state more painful, and heighten my apprehensions, and my opinion of the cruelty of the whites. One day they had taken a number of fishes; and when they had killed and satisfied themselves with as many as they thought fit, to our astonishment who were on the deck, rather than give any of them to us to eat, as we expected, they tossed the remaining fish into the sea again, although we begged and prayed for some as well as we could, but in vain; and some of my countrymen, being pressed by hunger, took an opportunity, when they thought no one saw them, of trying to get a little privately; but they were discovered, and the attempt procured them some very severe floggings.

One day, when we had a smooth sea, and moderate wind, two of my wearied countrymen, who were chained together (I was near them at the time), preferring death to such a life of misery, somehow made through the nettings, and jumped into the sea: immediately another quite dejected fellow, who, on account of his illness, was suffered to be out of irons, also followed their example; and I believe many more would very soon have done the same, if they had not been prevented by the ship's crew, who were instantly alarmed. Those of us that were the most active were, in a moment, put down under the deck; and there was such a noise and confusion amongst the people of the ship as I never heard before, to stop her, and get the boat out to go after the slaves. However, two of the wretches

81

were drowned, but they got the other, and afterwards flogged him unmer-cifully, for thus attempting to prefer death to slavery. In this manner we continued to undergo more hardships than I can now relate; hardships which are inseparable from this accursed trade.—Many a time we were near suffocation, from the want of fresh air, which we were often without for whole days together. This, and the stench of the necessary tubs, carried off many. During our passage I first saw flying fishes, which surprised me very much: they used frequently to fly across the ship, and many of them fell on the deck. I also now first saw the use of the quadrant.[11] I had often with astonishment seen the mariners make observations with it, and I could not think what it meant. They at last took notice of my surprise; and one of them, willing to increase it, as well as to gratify my curiosity, made me one day look through it. The clouds appeared to me to be land, which disappeared as they passed along. This heightened my wonder: and I was now more persuaded than ever that I was in another world, and that every thing about me was magic. At last we came in sight of the island of Barbadoes, at which the whites on board gave a great shout, and made many signs of joy to us. We did not know what to think of this; but as the vessel drew nearer we plainly saw the harbour, and other ships of differ-ent kinds and sizes: and we soon anchored amongst them off Bridge Town. Many merchants and planters now came on board, though it was in the evening. They put us in separate parcels,[12] and examined us attentively. They also made us jump,[13] and pointed to the land, signifying we were to go there. We thought by this we should be eaten by these ugly men, as they appeared to us; and, when soon after we were all put down under the deck again, there was much dread and trembling among us, and nothing but bit-ter cries to be heard all the night from these apprehensions, insomuch that at last the white people got some old slaves from the land to pacify us. They told us we were not to be eaten, but to work, and were soon to go on land, where we should see many of our country people. This report eased us much; and sure enough, soon after we were landed, there came to us Africans of all languages. We were conducted immediately to the mer-chant's yard, where we were all pent up together like so many sheep in a fold, without regard to sex or age. As every object was new to me, every thing I saw filled me with surprise. What struck me first was, that the houses were built with bricks, in stories,[14] and in every other respect different from those in I have seen in Africa:[15] but I was still more astonished on seeing people on horseback. I did not know what this could mean; and indeed I thought these people were full of nothing but magical arts. While I was in this astonishment, one of my fellow prisoners spoke to a countryman of his about the horses, who said they were the same kind they had in their country. I understood them, though they were from a distant part of Africa, and I thought it odd I had not seen any horses there; but afterwards, when I came to converse with different Africans, I found they had many horses amongst them, and much larger than those I then saw. We were not many days in the merchant's custody before we were sold after their usual manner, which is this:—On a signal given, (as the beat of a drum), the buyers rush at once into the yard where the slaves are confined, and make choice of that parcel they like best.[16] The noise and clamour with which this is attended, and the eagerness visible in the countenances of the buyers, serve not a little to increase the apprehensions of the terrified Africans, who may well be supposed to consider them as the ministers of that destruction to which they think themselves devoted.[17] In this manner, without scruple, are relations and friends separated, most of them never to see each other again. I remember in the vessel in which I was brought over, in the men's apartment, there were several brothers, who, in the sale, were sold in different lots; and it was very moving on this occasion to see and hear their cries at parting. O, ye nominal Christians! might not an African ask you, learned you this from your God? who says unto you, Do unto all men as you would men should do unto you? Is it not enough that we are torn from our country and friends to toil for your luxury and lust of gain? Must every tender feeling be likewise sacrificed to your avarice? Are the dearest friends and relations, now rendered more dear by their separation from their kindred, still to be parted from each other, and thus prevented from cheering the gloom of slavery with the small comfort of being together and mingling their sufferings and sorrows? Why are parents to lose their children, brothers their sisters, or husbands their wives? Surely this is a new refinement in cruelty, which, while it has no advantage to atone for it, thus aggravates distress, and adds fresh horrors even to the wretchedness of slavery.

83

END NOTES

1. Sound: healthy.
2. These two sentences were revised twice: the 1st ed. reads ". . . into terror when I was carried on board. I was immediately . . ."; the 3rd ed. reads ". . . into terror, which I am yet at a loss to describe; and the then feelings of my mind when carried on board. I was immediately . . ."; the final revision first appears in the 5th ed.
3. Long hair: only ed. 1 reads "loose hair."
4. Windlass: a winch, or crank, used to wind a heavy rope or chain to lift a weight.
5. Nettings: "a sort of fence, formed of an assemblage of ropes, fastened across each other" (William Falconer (1732–1769), *An Universal Dictionary of the Marine* [London, 1784; first published in 1769], hereafter cited in the notes as Falconer). These nettings were placed along the sides of the ship to form a caged enclosure to prevent the slaves from jumping overboard to try to escape or commit suicide.
6. The abolitionists frequently argued that the slave trade brutalized the enslavers as well as the enslaved. The tyrannical captain became almost a stock figure in the literature. The apologists for slavery argued that the trade served as a nursery for seamen. Evidence supports the abolitionists' claims that the trade was even more lethal, on an average percentage basis, for the crews than for the slaves. The Privy Council in 1789 estimated that the average mortality rate for slaves during the middle passage was 12.5 percent. Modern estimates of the mortality rate of 15 percent for slaves mean that of the approximately 10 million Africans taken to the Americas between 1600 and 1900, about 1.5 million died at sea. More than twice that number of African slaves died during the same period either while still in Africa or on their way to the Orient. The mortality rate of the much smaller number of marine slavers is estimated at about 20 percent. For both slaves and enslavers, the death rate varied with length of voyage, time, and age.
7. Foremast: the term *ship* was "particularly applied to a vessel furnished with three masts, each of which is composed of a lower mast, top mast, and top-gallant mast, with the usual machinery thereto belonging. The mast . . . placed at the middle of the ship's length, is called the main-mast, . . . that which is placed in the fore-part, the foremast, . . . and that which is towards the stem [the rear] is termed the mizen-mast" (Falconer).
8. Spell or magic: the anchor.
9. Boat: "a small open vessel, conducted on the water by rowing or sailing" (Falconer).
10. Necessary tubs: latrines.
11. Quadrant: "an instrument used to take the altitude of the sun or stars at sea, in order to determine the latitude of the place; or the sun's azimuth, so as to ascertain the magnetical variation" (Falconer).
12. Parcels: groups.
13. Made us jump: as a sign of health and strength.
14. The 1st ed. reads ". . . the houses were built with stories . . ."; the 2nd ed. reads ". . . the houses were built with bricks and stories . . ."; the final revision first appears in the 5th ed.
15. From . . . Africa: only ed. 1 reads "from those in Africa."
16. Equiano refers to what was known as the *scramble,* described from the perspective of an observer by Alexander Falconbridge (d. 1792) in *An Account of the Slave Trade on the Coast of Africa* (London, 1788):

> On a day appointed, the negroes were landed, and placed altogether in a large yard, belonging to the merchants to whom the ship was consigned. As soon

as the hour agreed on arrived, the doors of the yard were suddenly thrown open, and in rushed a considerable number of purchasers, with all the ferocity of brutes. Some instantly seized such of the negroes as they could conveniently lay hold of with their hands. Others, being prepared with several handkerchiefs tied together, encircled with these as many as they were able. While others, by means of a rope, effected the same purpose. It is scarcely possible to describe the confusion of which this mode of selling is productive. It likewise causes much animosity among the purchasers, who, not unfrequently upon these occasions, fall out and quarrel with each other. The poor astonished negroes were so much terrified by these proceedings, that several of them, through fear, climbed over the walls of the court yard, and ran wild about the town; but were soon hunted down and retaken (34).

Falconbridge's *Account* was written at the behest of the Society for Effecting the Abolition of the Slave Trade, which printed and distributed six thousand copies of it.
17. Devoted: doomed.

QUESTIONS

1. Equiano had encountered slavery in Africa, and he contrasts it to the slavery he experienced at the hands of the English. What contrasts does he draw?

2. What kind of language does Equiano use to describe his captors? What does he think of their behavior, not only to himself and other Africans, but to one another as well?

3. What account does Equiano give of slave sales?

4. How does Equiano use ideas—religious, social, and moral—embraced by the English to chastise them for the practice of slavery?

DOCUMENT

SLAVE IN A NEW WORLD

Aphra Behn

Aphra Behn was probably born in East Kent in 1640, but little is known about her origins and much of her later life remains shadowy. The authentic detail of her writing about Surinam lends support to Behn's claim that she was in the New World in 1664. A staunch Royalist, Behn traveled to the Low Countries in 1665 as a spy for Charles II, but was nearly thrown into debtor's prison after she failed to receive payment for her work. To support herself, Behn wrote prodigiously from 1670 until her death in 1689, producing poetry, Tory propaganda, short stories, stage plays, and novels. She boasted that she had written Oroonoko, which remains her best known work, in a few hours. Though Behn's strong political opinions and "female pen" made her the target of harsh satire, her talent was recognized by contemporaries such as Dryden, and she was hailed as an important influence by later writers, most notably Virginia Woolf.

Styled as the travel narrative of an Englishwoman in the sugar colony of Surinam during the early 1660s, much of Oroonoko is devoted to relating the story of a heroic African prince who is enslaved and taken to the New World, where he is executed after leading a slave uprising. First published in 1688, the novel's compassionate treatment of its Black hero and its indictment of slavery made it a favorite of reformers for more than a century after Behn's death. Here, Oroonoko, renamed Caesar by his master Mr. Trefy, conspires to regain liberty for himself, his wife Imoinda, and his fellow slaves.

Reprinted from *Oroonoko, The Rover, and Other Works*, 1668.

[N]ow Imoinda began to show she was with child, and did nothing but sigh and weep for the captivity of her lord, herself, and the infant yet unborn, and believed, if it were so hard to gain the liberty of two, 'twould be more difficult to get that for three. Her griefs were so many darts in the great heart of Caesar, and taking his opportunity one Sunday, when all the whites were overtaken with drink he went pretending out of goodness to them, to feast amongst them, and sent all his music, and ordered a great treat for the whole gang, about three hundred Negroes. And about a hundred and fifty were able to bear arms, such as they had, which were sufficient to do execution with spirits accordingly. For the English had none but rusty swords, that no strength could draw from a scabbard, except the people of particular quality, who took care to oil them and keep them in good order. The guns also, unless here and there one, or those newly carried from England, would do no good or harm, for 'tis the nature of that county to rust and eat up iron, or any metals, but gold and silver. And they are very inexpert at the bow, which the Negroes and Indians are perfect masters of.

Caesar, having singled out these men from the women and children, made a harangue to them of the miseries, and ignominies of slavery; counting up all their toils and sufferings, under such loads, burdens, and drudgeries, as were fitter for beasts than men; senseless brutes, than human souls. He told them it was not for days, months, or years, but for eternity; there was no end to be of their misfortunes. They suffered not like men who might find a glory, and fortitude in oppression, but like dogs that loved the whip and bell,[1] and fawned the more they were beaten. That they had lost the divine quality of men, and were become insensible asses, fit only to bear. Nay worse, an ass, or dog, or horse having done his duty, could lie down in retreat, and rise to work again, and while he did his duty endured no stripes, but men, villainous, senseless men, such as they, toiled on all the tedious week till black Friday, and then, whether they worked or not, whether they were faulty or meriting, they promiscuously, the innocent with the guilty, suffered the infamous whip, the sordid stripes, from their fellow slaves till their blood trickled from all parts of their body, blood whose every drop ought to be revenged with a life of some of those tyrants that impose it. 'And why,' said he, 'my dear friends and fellow sufferers, should we be slaves to an unknown people? Have they vanquished us nobly in fight? Have they won us in honourable battle? And are we, by the chance of war, become their slaves? This would not anger a noble heart, this would not animate a soldier's soul. No, but we are bought and sold like apes, or monkeys, to be the sport of women, fools and cowards, and the support of rogues, runagades,[2] that have abandoned their own countries, for raping, murders, thefts and villainies. Do you not hear every day how they upbraid each other with infamy of life, below the wildest salvages,[3] and shall we render obedience to such a degenerate race, who have no one human virtue left, to distinguish them from the vilest creatures? Will you, I say, suffer the lash from such hands?'[4] They all replied, with one accord, 'No, no, no; Caesar had spoke like a great captain, like a great king.'

After this he would have proceeded, but was interrupted by a tall Negro of some more quality than the rest. His name was Tuscan, who bowing at the feet of Caesar, cried, 'My lord, we have listened with joy and attention to what you have said, and, were we only men, would follow so great a leader through the world. But oh! consider, we are husbands and parents too, and have things more dear to us than life: our wives and children unfit for travel, in these impassable woods, mountains and bogs. We have not only difficult lands to overcome, but rivers to wade, and monsters to encounter, ravenous beasts of prey—' To this, Caesar replied, that honour was the first principle in Nature that was to be obeyed; but as no man would pretend to that, without all the acts of virtue, compassion, charity, love, justice and reason, he found it not inconsistent with that, to take an equal care of their wives and children, as they would of themselves, and that he did not design, when he led them to freedom, and glorious liberty, that they should leave that better part of themselves to perish by the hand of the tyrant's whip. But if there were a woman among them so degenerate from love and virtue to choose slavery before the pursuit of her husband, and with the hazard of her life, to share with him in his fortunes, that such an one ought to be abandoned, and left as a prey to the common enemy.

To which they all agreed—and bowed. After this, he spoke of the impassable woods and rivers, and convinced them, the more danger, the more glory. He told them that he had heard of one Hannibal a great captain, had cut his way through mountains of solid rocks,[5] and should a few shrubs oppose them, which they could fire before them? No, 'twas a trifling excuse to men resolved to die, or overcome. As for bogs, they are with a little labour filled and hardened, and the rivers could be no obstacle, since they swam by nature, at least by custom, from their first hour of their birth. That when the children were weary they must carry them by turns, and the woods and their own industry would afford them food. To this they all assented with joy.

Tuscan then demanded, what he would do? He said, they would travel towards the sea; plant a new colony, and defend it by their valour; and when they could find a ship, either driven by stress of weather, or guided by providence that way, they would seize it, and make it a prize, till it had transported them to their own countries. At least, they should be made free in his kingdom, and be esteemed as his fellow sufferers, and men that had the courage, and the bravery to attempt, at least, for liberty. And if they died in the attempt it would be more brave, than to live in perpetual slavery.

They bowed and kissed his feet at this resolution, and with one accord vowed to follow him to death. And that night was appointed to begin their march; they made it known to their wives, and directed them to tie their hamaca[6] about their shoulder, and under their arm like a scarf; and to lead their children that could go, and carry those that could not. The wives who pay an entire obedience to their husbands obeyed, and stayed for them, where they were appointed. The men stayed but to furnish themselves with what defensive arms they could get, and all met at the rendezvous, where Caesar made a new encouraging speech to them, and led them out.

But, as they could not march far that night, on Monday early, when the overseers went to call them all together, to go to work, they were extremely surprised to find not one upon the place, but all fled with what baggage they had. You may imagine this news was not only suddenly spread all over the plantation, but soon reached the neighbouring ones, and we had by noon about six hundred men, they call the militia of the county, that came to assist us in the pursuit of the fugitives. But never did one see so comical an army march forth to war. The men, of any fashion, would not concern themselves, though it were almost the common cause, for such revoltings are very ill examples, and have very fatal consequences oftentimes in many colonies. But they had a respect for Caesar, . . .

because they did not, in the first place, love the Lord Governor, and secondly, they would have it, that Caesar was ill used, and baffled with.[7] And 'tis not impossible but some of the best in the country was of his counsel in this flight, and depriving us of all the slaves, so that they of the better sort would not meddle in the matter. The deputy governor, of whom I have had no great occasion to speak, and who was the most fawning fair-tongued fellow in the world, and one that pretended the most friendship to Caesar, was now the only violent man against him, and though he had nothing, and so need fear nothing, yet talked and looked bigger than any man. He was a fellow, whose character is not fit to be mentioned with the worst of the slaves. This fellow would lead his army forth to meet Caesar, or rather to pursue him. Most of their arms were of those sort of cruel whips they call cat with nine tails;[8] some had rusty useless guns for show; others old basket-hilts, whose blades had never seen the light in this age, and others had long staffs, and clubs. Mr Trefry went along, rather to be a mediator than a conqueror, in such a battle; for he foresaw, and knew, if by fighting they put the Negroes into despair, they were a sort of sullen fellows, that would drown, or kill themselves, before they would yield, and he advised that fair means was best. But Byam[9] was one that abounded in his own wit, and would take his own measures.

It was not hard to find these fugitives, for as they fled they were forced to fire and cut the woods before them, so that night or day they pursued them by the light they made, and by the path they had cleared. But as soon as Caesar found he was pursued, he put himself in a posture of defence, placing all the women and children in the rear, and himself, with Tuscan by his side, or next to him, all promising to die or conquer. Encouraged thus, they never stood to parley, but fell on pell-mell upon the English, and killed some, and wounded a good many, they having recourse to their whips, as the best of their weapons. And as they observed no order, they perplexed the enemy so sorely, with lashing them in the eyes. And the women and children, seeing their husbands so treated, being of fearful cowardly dispositions, and hearing the English cry out, 'Yield and live, yield and be pardoned', they all ran in amongst their husbands and fathers, and hung about them, crying out, 'Yield, yield, and leave Caesar to their revenge', that by degrees the slaves abandoned Caesar, and left him only Tuscan and his heroic Imoinda, who, grown big as she was, did nevertheless press near her lord, having a bow, and a quiver full of poisoned arrows, which she managed with such dexterity, that she wounded several, and shot the governor into the shoulder, of which wound he had like to have died, but that an Indian woman, his mistress, sucked the wound, and cleansed it from the venom. But however, he stirred not from the place till he had parlied with Caesar, who he found was resolved to die fighting, and would not be taken; no more would Tuscan, or Imoinda. But he, more thirsting after revenge of another sort, than that of depriving him of life, now made use of all his art of talking, and dissembling, and besought Caesar to yield himself upon terms, which he himself should propose, and should be sacredly assented to and kept by him. He told him, it was not that he any longer feared him, or could believe the force of two men, and a young heroine, could overcome all them, with all the slaves now on their side also, but it was the vast esteem he had for his person, the desire he had to serve so gallant a man, and to hinder himself from the reproach hereafter, of having been the occasion of the death of a prince, whose valour and magnanimity deserved the empire of the world. He protested to him, he looked upon this action, as gallant and brave, however tending to the prejudice of his lord and master, who would by it have lost so considerable a number of slaves, that this flight of his should be looked on as a heat of youth, and rashness of a too forward courage, and an unconsidered impatience of liberty, and no more; and that he laboured in vain to accomplish that which they would effectually perform, as soon as any ship arrived that would touch on his coast. 'So that if you will be pleased,' continued he, 'to surrender yourself, all imaginable respect shall be paid you; and yourself, your wife, and child, if it be here born, shall depart free out of our land.' But Caesar would hear of no composition, though Byam urged, if he pursued, and went on in his design, he would inevitably perish, either by great snakes, wild beasts, or hunger, and he ought to have regard to his wife, whose condition required ease, and not the fatigues of tedious travel, where she could not be secured from being devoured. But Caesar told him, there was no faith in the white men, or the gods they adored, who instructed them in principles so false, that honest men could not live amongst them; though no people professed so much, none performed so little; that he knew what he had to do, when he dealt with men of honour, but with them a man ought to be eternally on his guard, and never to eat and drink with Christians without his weapon of defence in his hand, and, for his own security, never to credit one word they spoke. As for the rashness and inconsiderateness of his action he would confess the governor is in the right, and that he was ashamed of what he had done, in endeavouring to make those free, who were by nature slaves, poor wretched rogues, fit to be used as Christians' tools; dogs, treacherous and cowardly, fit for such masters, and they wanted only but to be whipped into the knowledge of the Christian gods to be the vilest of all creeping things, to learn to worship such deities as had not power to make them just, brave, or honest. In fine, after a thousand things of this nature, not fit here to be recited, he told Byam, he had rather die than live upon the same earth with such dogs. But Trefry and Byam pleaded and protested together so much, that Trefry believing the governor to mean what he said, and speaking very cordially himself, generously put himself into Caesar's hands, and took him aside, and persuaded him, even with tears, to live, by surrendering himself, and to name his conditions. Caesar was overcome by his wit and reasons, and in consideration of Imoinda, and demanding what he desired, and that it should be ratified by their hands in writing, because he had perceived that was the common way of contract between man and man, amongst the whites. All this was performed, and Tuscan's pardon was put in, and they surrender to the governor, who walked peaceably down into the plantation with them, after giving order to bury their dead. Caesar was very much toiled with the bustle of the day, for he had fought like a Fury, and what mischief was done he and Tuscan performed alone, and gave their enemies a fatal proof that they durst do anything, and feared no mortal force.

But they were no sooner arrived at the place, where all the slaves receive their punishments of whipping, but they laid hands on Caesar and Tuscan, faint with heat and toil; and, surprising them, bound them to two several stakes, and whipped them in a most deplorable and inhumane manner, rending the very flesh from their bones; especially Caesar, who was not perceived to make any moan, or to alter his face, only to roll his eyes on the faithless governor, and those he believed guilty, with fierceness and indignation. And, to complete his rage, he saw every one of those slaves, who, but a few days before, adored him as something more than mortal, now had a whip to give him some lashes, while he strove not to break his fetters, though, if he had, it were impossible. But he pronounced a woe and revenge from his eyes, that darted fire, that 'twas at once both awful and terrible to behold.[10]

When they thought they were sufficiently revenged on him, they untied him, almost fainting, with loss of blood, from a thousand wounds all over his body, from which they had rent his clothes, and led him bleeding and naked as he was, and loaded him all over with irons, and then rubbed his wounds, to complete their cruelty, with Indian pepper, which had like to have made him raving mad, and, in this condition, made him so fast to the ground that he could not stir, if his pains and wounds would have given him leave. They spared Imoinda, and did not let her see this barbarity committed towards her lord, but carried her down to Parham, and shut her up, which was not in kindness to her, but for fear she should die with the sight, or miscarry, and then they should lose a young slave, and perhaps the mother.

. . .

The governor was no sooner recovered, and had heard of the menaces of Caesar, but he called his council, who (not to disgrace them, or burlesque the government there) consisted of such notorious villains as Newgate[11] never transported, and possibly originally were such, who understood neither the laws of God or man, and had no sort of principles to make them worthy the name of men. But, at the very council table, would contradict and fight with one another, and swear so bloodily that 'twas terrible to hear, and see them. (Some of them were afterwards hanged, when the Dutch took possession of the place; others sent off in chains.) But calling these special rulers of the nation together, and requiring their counsel in this weighty affair, they all concluded, that (damn them) it might be their own cases, and that Caesar ought to be made an example to all the Negroes, to fright them from daring to threaten their betters, their lords and masters, and, at this rate, no man was safe from his own slaves, and concluded, *nemine contradicente*,[12] that Caesar should be hanged.

. . .

[T]he governor . . . communicated his design to one Banister,[13] a wild Irishman, and one of the council, a fellow of absolute barbarity, and fit to execute any villainy, but was rich. He came up to Parham, and forcibly took Caesar, and had him carried to the same post where he was whipped, and causing him to be tied to it, and a great fire made before him, he told him, he should die like a dog, as he was. Caesar replied, this was the first piece of bravery that ever Banister did, and he never spoke sense till he pronounced that word, and, if he would keep it, he would declare, in the other world, that he was the only man, of all the whites, that ever he heard speak truth. And turning to the men that bound him, he said, 'My friends, am I to die, or to be whipped?' And they cried, 'Whipped! no; you shall not escape so well.' And then he replied, smiling, 'A blessing on thee', and assured them, they need not tie him, for he would stand fixed, like a rock, and endure death so as should encourage them to die. 'But if you whip me,' said he, 'be sure you tie me fast.'

He had learned to take tobacco, and when he was assured he should die, he desired they would give him a pipe in his mouth, ready lighted, which they did,[14] and the executioner came, and first cut off his members, and threw them into the fire. After that, with an ill-favoured knife, they cut his ears, and his nose, and burned them; he still smoked on, as if nothing had touched him. Then they hacked off one of his arms, and still he bore up, and held his pipe. But at the cutting off the other arm, his head sunk, and his pipe dropped, and he gave up the ghost, without a groan, or a reproach. My mother and sister were by him all the while, but not suffered to save him, so rude and wild were the rabble, and so inhuman were the justices, who stood by to see the execution, who after paid dearly enough for their insolence. They cut Caesar in quarters, and sent them to several of the chief plantations. One quarter was sent to Colonel Martin, who refused it, and swore, he had rather see the quarters of Banister, and the governor himself, than those of Caesar, on his plantations, and that he could govern his Negroes without terrifying and grieving them with frightful spectacles of a mangled king.

Thus died this great man, worthy of a better fate, and a more sublime wit than mine to write his praise. Yet, I hope, the reputation of my pen is considerable enough to make his glorious name to survive to all ages, with that of the brave, the beautiful, and the constant Imoinda.

END NOTES

1. 'Something that detracts from one's comfort or pleasure' (*O.E.D.*).
2. Renegades; apostates and deserters.
3. Savages
4. Southerne, who was impressed with Behn's dramatic presentation of *Oroonoko* and had wondered why she did not herself make the story into a play, makes Oroonoko speak in black verse on heroic occasions such as this and differentiates him more sharply than Behn from the other blacks.
5. When crossing the Alps, 'in certaine places of the highest rockes, [Hannibal] was driven to make passage through, by force of fire and vinegar' (Plutarch, *The Lives of the Noble Grecians and Romanes,* North's translation, 1579 edition).
6. Hammock, from the Carib word through Spanish *hamaca.* Pepys comments on buying 'hammacoes' for the navy.
7. Deceived and abused.
8. Whip with nine knotted lashes used in the British navy and army.
9. William Byam was the royalist governor of Surinam from c.1654 and then deputy governor under Willoughby. In 1663 he became lieutenant general, a position the narrator claims her father should have held.
10. Behn was contemptuous of turncoats, especially when they were disloyal to her respected James II, from whom support was slipping away during 1688.
11. A London prison from which many convicts were exported to work on New World plantations. For example, in 1681 Christopher Jeaffreson bought 300 convicts from the chief gaoler of Newgate to use on his plantation in Jamaica. See also Behn, *The Widow Ranter.*
12. Unanimously
13. Major James Bannister. In 1688, after the Treaty of Breda, he negotiated with the Dutch on behalf of the remaining English settlers and was sent as a prisoner to Holland.
14. See Bryan Edwards and John Stedman, *Narrative of a Five Years' Expedition Against the Revolted Negroes of Surinam* (1796) for a later description of a tortured man smoking a pipe of tobacco.

QUESTIONS

1. Why do the other slaves follow Caesar in rebellion? What personal qualities does he show that convinces them to join the struggle?

2. How does Behn depict most of the leaders of plantation society? What is her estimation of their morality?

3. How, in Behn's account, does slavery debase both slaves and slave-holders?

4. Behn writes of people of many different races and nations. What does she think of these differences? Are these, according to Behn, the most important determinants of individual character?

DOCUMENT

THE VIEW OF OSEI BONSU

Joseph Dupuis

*Joseph Dupuis headed the second British diplomatic mission to Asante in
1820, a follow-up on a previous mission to Kingdom of Asante in 1817 under
the leadership of Thomas Edward Bowdich. Both missions resulted in substantial publications about Asante authored by contemporary diplomatic
heads, and these constitute some of the earliest accounts on the kingdom at
the beginning of the nineteenth century. Asante emerged as a state around
1701 after the military defeat of its overlord Denkyira. It went on to expand
territorially to incorporate an area larger than present-day Ghana. In the
process, Asante became a major slave trader as well as a slave-holding society. The abolition of the slave trade by Denmark in 1803 and the British in
1807, two of the three main European nations trading on the Gold Coast at
the beginning of the nineteenth century, created a temporary crisis for Asante.
The increase in unsold slaves in the capital city of Kumasi and the prospect of
an emergent underclass created by the merging of the poor and servile classes
caused the Asante aristocracy great unease. HRH Osei Bonsu was the
Asantehene (King of the Ashanti), reigning from 1804 to 1824. He used the
occasion of the Dupuis mission to petition unsuccessfully for the British re-
opening of the export slave trade.*

"Now," said the king, after a pause, "I have another palaver, and you must
help me to talk it. A long time ago the great king liked plenty of trade,
more than now; then many ships came, and they bought ivory, gold, and

Reprinted from *Journal of a Residence in Ashantee,* 1824.

slaves; but now he will not let the ships come as before, and the people buy gold and ivory only. This is what I have in my head, so now tell me truly, like a friend, why does the king do so?" "His majesty's question," I replied, "was connected with a great palaver, which my instructions did not authorise me to discuss. I had nothing to say regarding the slave trade." "I know that too," retorted the king; "because, if my master liked that trade, you would have told me so before. I only want to hear what you think as a friend: this is not like the other palavers." I was confessedly at a loss for an argument that might pass as a satisfactory reason, and the sequel proved that my doubts were not groundless. The king did not deem it plausible, that this obnoxious traffic should have been abolished from motives of humanity alone; neither would he admit that it lessened the number either of domestic or foreign wars.

Taking up one of my observations, he remarked, "the white men who go to council with your master, and pray to the great God for him, do not understand my country, or they would not say the slave trade was bad. But if they think it bad now, why did they think it good before. Is not your law an old law, the same as the Crammo[1] law? Do you not both serve the same God, only you have different fashions and customs? Crammos are strong people in fetische, and they say the law is good, because the great God made the book; so they buy slaves, and teach them good things, which they knew not before. This makes every body love the Crammos, and they go every where up and down, and the people give them food when they want it. Then these men come all the way from the great water[2], and from Manding, and Dagomba, and Killinga; they stop and trade for slaves, and then go home. If the great king would like to restore this trade, it would be good for the white men and for me too, because Ashantee is a country for war, and the people are strong; so if you talk that palaver for me properly, in the white country, if you go there, I will give you plenty of gold, and I will make you richer than all the white men."

I urged the impossibility of the king's request, promising, however, to record his sentiments faithfully. "Well then," said the king, "you must put down in my master's book all I shall say, and then he will look to it, now he is my friend. And when he sees what is true, he will surely restore that trade. I cannot make war to catch slaves in the bush, like a thief. My ancestors never did so. But if I fight a king, and kill him when he is insolent, then certainly I must have his gold, and his slaves, and the people are mine too. Do not the white kings act like this? Because I hear the old men say, that before I conquered Fantee and killed the Braffoes and the kings, that white men came in great ships, and fought and killed many people; and then they took the gold and slaves to the white country: and sometimes they fought together. That is all the same as these black countries. The great God and the fetische made war for strong men every where, because then they can pay plenty of gold and proper sacrifice. When I fought Gaman, I did not make war for slaves, but because Dinkera (the king) sent me an arrogant message and killed my people, and refused to pay me gold as his father did. Then my fetische made me strong like my ancestors, and I killed Dinkera, and took his gold, and brought more than 20,000 slaves to Coomassy. Some of these people being bad men, I washed my stool in their blood for the fetische. But then some were good people, and these I sold or gave to my captains: many, moreover, died, because this country does not grow too much corn like Sarem, and what can I do? Unless I kill or sell them, they will grow strong and kill my people. Now you must tell my master that these slaves can work for him, and if he wants 10,000 he can have them. And if he wants fine handsome girls and women to give his captains, I can send him great numbers."

The wars of the king were shortly after introduced as a topic of general discussion. That of Gaman was the favourite subject, and the king occasionally took up the thread of the narrative, or elucidated such events as were perhaps not generally known. As he caused the linguists to interpret to me the particular feats of himself, the king of Banna and Apoko, his eyes sparkled with fiery animation, and at one period he threw himself into a sort of theatrical attitude, which appeared to be unpremeditated, and unaffected. He then seemed to be wrapped up within, himself in delightful cogitations, and at this crisis, some of the auditors like the bards of "olden time," rose to the hum of the war song, and recited their parts in a pleasing mellifluous strain. The king enjoyed the scene in extacy, and frequently motioned with his body and feet in cadence with the metre of the verse. This reverie and the recitation occupied many minutes, and were ultimately succeeded by irony and satire cast upon the memory of his fallen enemy. "His scull was broken," said the king, "but I would not lose the trophy, and now I have made a similar scull of gold. This is for my great customs, that all the people may know *I* am the king."

A slave was deputed to one of the apartments of the palace, and as he returned he deposited a chair,[3] which his majesty said was the regal seat of Dinkera. This piece of workmanship was studded all over with gold and silver ornaments, and silver coin of different European states. The slave again disappeared, and returned, bringing under his escort a son of that unfortunate monarch, one of the few male survivors of the race of Dinkera. A pallid hue, if so it may be termed, overspread the jetty features of the youth, as he bowed trembling before the king. The angry glance which marked his reception, excited the most painful apprehensions, and the countenance of the young man spoke woeful agony, as he endeavoured to scan the purport of the summons.

"Your father," said the king, addressing himself to the prince. "was a rebel; he was full of pride, and wanted to be a great king; he forgot when he was my slave. Is not this true? Then he wanted Sarem to help him, and sent gold to make friends. Is not that true, too? He forgot I was his master; he killed my sword bearers, and sent me an insulting message. Now I have his scull, and the jaw bones of his captains. His wives, and you, and all the people are my slaves; and when I tell you to die, you shall die as your brother did; but now you shall serve me."

The king then desired him to strip off his robe and shew me the wounds he had received in battle. The unhappy youth did as he was instructed, pointing to five or six honourable scars upon his breast, arms, and thighs, which had the appearance of gun-shot wounds. "Now," said the king to him, with a stern, sarcastic apathy, "you know your father was a fool, and that I am the king; you did not know that before; and so now go home until I send for you again."[4]

END NOTES

1. Moslem law.
2. Niger.
3. The stool or chair is esteemed the throne. It denotes supremacy and sovereignty in rank, not only in Ashantee, but in most eastern nations, as well as the states of Morocco, Algiers, Tunis, &c.
4. This illustrious prisoner was placed under the safeguard of an inferior captain, who employed him in work at his plantations. The negro has no tender sentiment for his

humbled antagonist! He was compelled, in the presence of the king, to join a chorus in the cruel *Epicedium*, or death-song, which preceded his brother's sacrifice :—an execution which was performed in his presence, with torture, and amidst the mockery and derision of the whole court.

QUESTIONS

1. Why was Osei Bonsu puzzled by the British abolition of the export slave trade?
2. What other commodities had been exported historically from the Gold Coast?
3. How did Osei Bonsu justify the continuation of the slave trade?
4. What did you learn about the nature of power in Asante from Osei Bonsu's description of his prerogatives as king?

Nineteenth-Century Imperialism

TRAVELS IN WEST AFRICA

Mary Kingsley

Mary Kingsley was born in 1862 and spent the first thirty years of her life in the quiet comfort of the English countryside. After the death of her parents, however, she broke with Victorian custom by traveling alone through remote parts of Africa. Her initial intent was to continue her father's study of religious fetishes, but she later expanded her focus to include the collection of scientific specimens and the mapping of unexplored inland regions. She made two extensive journeys in West and West Central Africa, and scaled Mt. Cameroon, one of the tallest mountains on the continent. Her explorations were cut short by her death at age thirty-eight during the Boer War in South Africa.

Kingsley's Travels in West Africa, *published in 1897, is her best-known work. Based on her journal entries, it outlines her experiences and observations during her two major journeys. The book caused controversy because of Kingsley's vocal disapproval of the economic expropriation undertaken by European colonial regimes. Her distaste for imperial exploitation reflected a new and critical view of late-nineteenth century colonialism and foreshadowed the turn of the century scandals surrounding the Belgian Congo.*

⋯⋯⋯⋯

I, with my crew, keep on up the grand new road the Government is making, which when finished is to go from Ambas Bay to Buea, 3,000 feet up on the mountain's side. This road is quite the most magnificent of roads,

Reprinted from *Travels in West Africa*, 1897.

as regards breadth and general intention, that I have seen anywhere in West Africa, and it runs through a superbly beautiful country. It is, I should say, as broad as Oxford Street; on either side of it are deep drains to carry off the surface waters, with banks of varied beautiful tropical shrubs and ferns, behind which rise, 100 to 200 feet high, walls of grand forest, the column-like tree-stems either hung with flowering, climbing plants and ferns, or showing soft red and soft grey shafts sixty to seventy feet high without an interrupting branch. Behind this again rise the lovely foot hills of Mungo, high up against the sky, coloured the most perfect soft dark blue.

The whole scheme of colour is indescribably rich and full in tone. The very earth is a velvety red brown, and the butterflies—which abound—show themselves off in the sunlight, in their canary-coloured, crimson, and peacock-blue liveries, to perfection. After five minutes' experience of the road I envy those butterflies. I do not believe there is a more lovely road in this world, and besides, it's a noble and enterprising thing of a Government to go and make it, considering the climate and the country; but to get any genuine pleasure out of it, it is requisite to hover in a bird- or butterfly-like way, for of all the truly awful things to walk on, that road, when I was on it, was the worst.

Of course this arose from its not being finished, not having its top on in fact: the bit that was finished, and had got its top on, for half a mile beyond the bridge, you could go over in a Bath chair. The rest of it made you fit for one for the rest of your natural life, for it was one mass of broken lava rock, and here and there leviathan tree-stumps that had been partially blown up with gunpowder.

When we near the forest end of the road, it comes on to rain heavily, and I see a little house on the left-hand side, and a European engineer superintending a group of very cheerful natives felling timber. He most kindly invites me to take shelter, saying it cannot rain as heavily as this for long. My men also announce a desire for water, and so I sit down and chat with the engineer under the shelter of his verandah, while the men go to the water-hole, some twenty minutes off.

The engineer is an Alsatian, and has been engaged on the Congo Free State Railway, which he abandoned because they put him up at the end station, on those awful Palaballa mountains. Four men who were at the station died of fever and he got it himself, and applied for leave to go down to Matadi to see a doctor. His request was peremptorily refused, and he was told he must remain at his post until another engineer came up to take over charge. He stayed for some days waiting, but no one came or gave signs of coming, and he found the company had given all their employees orders that he was not to be allowed on a train, so he walked down to Matadi. How he did it, knowing that country, I cannot think, but he was exceedingly ill when he got there, as may easily be imagined, and as soon as he had sufficiently recovered, he came up to Cameroons, and obtained his present appointment, after having been kept and nursed up in the hospital there, to his considerable surprise after his Congo experiences. He was not hopeful about the future of that Congo railroad, or of that of its directors. He quoted as one of the reasons for his leaving it the doubt that it would ever be finished. Inexplicable is man! Why he should have cared whether it was finished or not as long as it kept on paying him £1 a day, I do not know. He had kept a diary of the accidents, which averaged two a day, and usually took the form of something going off the line, because the railway engines used were so light as to be flighty, and not really powerful enough to take up more than two trucks at a time, though always expected to do so. The wages of the natives employed were from 1s. to 1s. 6d. a day; very high pay. The Chinamen imported as navvies were an awful nuisance, always making palaver. The Senegal men are dangerous, because the French officials on the line always support them against other white men, Senegalese being Frenchmen, just as Kruboys are Englishmen.

While I am getting this last news from Congo, the rain keeps on pouring down. I presently see one of my men sitting right in the middle of the road on a rock, totally unsheltered, and a feeling of shame comes over me in the face of this black man's aquatic courage. Besides, Herr von Lucke had said I was sure to get half-drowned and catch an awful cold, so there is no use delaying. Into the rain I go, and off we start. I may remark I subsequently found that my aquatic underling was drunk. I conscientiously attempt to keep dry, by holding up an umbrella, knowing that though hopeless it is the proper thing to do.

We leave the road about fifty yards above the hut, turning into the unbroken forest on the right-hand side, and following a narrow, slippery, muddy, root-beset bush-path that was a comfort after the road. Presently we come to a lovely mountain torrent flying down over red-brown rocks in white foam; exquisitely lovely, and only a shade damper than the rest of things. Seeing this I solemnly fold up my umbrella and give it to Kefalla. My relations, nay, even Mrs. Roy, who is blind to a large percentage of my imperfections, say the most scathing things about my behaviour with regard to water. But really my conduct is founded on sound principles. I know from a series of carefully conducted experiments, carried out on the Devonshire Lynn, that I cannot go across a river on slippery stepping-stones; therefore, knowing that attempts to keep my feet out of water only end in my placing the rest of my anatomy violently in, I take charge of Fate and wade.

This particular stream, too, requires careful wading, the rocks over which it flows being arranged in picturesque, but perilous confusion; however all goes well, and getting to the other side I decide to "chuck it," as Captain Davis would say, as to keeping dry, for the rain comes down heavier than ever.

Now we are evidently dealing with a foot-hillside, but the rain is too thick for one to see two yards in any direction, and we seem to be in a ghost-land forest, for the great palms and red-woods rise up in the mist before us, and fade out in the mist behind, as we pass on. The rocks which edge and strew the path at our feet are covered with exquisite ferns and mosses—all the most delicate shades of green imaginable, and here and there of absolute gold colour, looking as if some ray of sunshine had lingered too long playing on the earth, and had got shut off from heaven by the mist, and so lay nestling among the rocks until it might rejoin the sun.

The path now becomes an absolute torrent, with mud-thickened water, which cascades round one's ankles in a sportive way, and round one's knees in the hollows in the path. Five seconds after abandoning the umbrella I am wet through, but it is not uncomfortable at this temperature, something like that of a cucumber frame with the lights on, if you can clear your mind of all prejudice, as Dr. Johnson says, and forget the risk of fever which saturation entails.

On we go, the path underneath the water seems a pretty equal mixture of rock and mud, but they are not evenly distributed. Plantations full of weeds show up on either side of us, and we are evidently now on the top

106

of a foot-hill. I suspect a fine view of the sea could be obtained from here, if you have an atmosphere that is less than 99¾ per cent. of water. As it is, a white sheet—or more properly speaking, considering its soft, stuffy woolliness, a white blanket—is stretched across the landscape to the south-west, where the sea would show.

We go down-hill now, the water rushing into the back of my shoes for a change. The path is fringed by high, sugar-cane-like grass which hangs across it in a lackadaisical way, swishing you in the face and cutting like a knife whenever you catch its edge, and pouring continually insidious rills of water down one's neck. It does not matter. The whole Atlantic could not get more water on to me than I have already got. Ever and again I stop and wring out some of it from my skirts, for it is weighty. One would not imagine that anything could come down in the way of water thicker than the rain, but it can. When one is on the top of the hills, a cold breeze comes through the mist chilling one to the bone, and bending the heads of the palm trees, sends down from them water by the bucketful with a slap; hitting or missing you as the case may be.

Both myself and my men are by now getting anxious for our "chop," and they tell me, "We look them big hut soon." Soon we do look them big hut, but with faces of undisguised horror, for the big hut consists of a few charred roof-mats, &c., lying on the ground. There has been a fire in that simple savage home. Our path here is cut by one that goes east and west, and after a consultation between my men and the Bakwiri, we take the path going east, down a steep slope between weedy plantations, and shortly on the left shows a steep little hill-side with a long low hut on the top. We go up to it and I find it is the habitation of a Basel Mission black Bible-reader. He comes out and speaks English well, and I tell him I want a house for myself and my men, and he says we had better come and stay in this one. It is divided into two chambers, one in which the children who attend the mission-school stay, and wherein there is a fire, and one evidently the abode of the teacher. I thank the Bible-reader and say that I will pay him for the house, and I and the men go in streaming, and my teeth chatter with cold as the breeze chills my saturated garment while I give out the rations of beef, rum, blankets, and tobacco to the men. Then I clear my apartment out and attempt to get dry, operations which are interrupted by Kefalla coming for tobacco to buy firewood off the mission teacher to cook our food by.

Presently my excellent little cook brings in my food, and in with it come two mission teachers—our first acquaintance, the one with a white jacket, and another with a blue. They lounge about and spit in all directions, and then chiefs commence to arrive with their families complete, and they sidle into the apartment and ostentatiously ogle the demi-john of rum.

They are, as usual, a nuisance, sitting about on everything. No sooner have I taken an unclean-looking chief off the wood sofa, than I observe another one has silently seated himself in the middle of my open portmanteau. Removing him and shutting it up, I see another one has settled on the men's beef and rice sack.

It is now about three o'clock and I am still chilled to the bone in spite of tea. The weather is as bad as ever. The men say that the rest of the road to Buea is far worse than that which we have so far come along, and that we should never get there before dark, and "for sure" should not get there afterwards, because by the time the dark came down we should be in "bad place too much." Therefore, to their great relief, I say I will stay at this place—Buana—for the night, and go on in the morning time up to Buea; and just for the present I think I will wrap myself up in a blanket and try and get the chill out of me, so I give the chiefs a glass of rum each, plenty of head tobacco, and my best thanks for their kind call, and then turn them and the expectorating mission teachers out. I have not been lying down five minutes on the plank that serves for a sofa by day and a bed by night, when Charles comes knocking at the door. He wants tobacco. "Missionary man no fit to let we have firewood unless we buy em." Give Charles a head and shut him out again, and drop off to sleep again for a quarter of an hour, then am aroused by some enterprising sightseers pushing open the window-shutters; when I look round there are a mass of black heads sticking through the window-hole. I tell them respectfully that the circus is closed for repairs, and fasten up the shutters, but sleep is impossible, so I turn out and go and see what those men of mine are after. They are comfortable enough round their fire, with their clothes suspended on strings in the smoke above them, and I envy them that fire. I then stroll round to see if there is anything to be seen, but the scenery is much like that you would enjoy if you were inside a blancmange. So as it is now growing dark I return to my room and light candles, and read Dr. Günther on Fishes. If this sort of weather goes on I expect I shall specialise fins and gills myself. Room becomes full of blacks. Unless you watch the door, you do not see how it is done. You look at a corner one minute and it is empty, and the next time you look that way it is full of rows of white teeth and watching eyes. The two mission teachers come in and make a show of teaching a child to read the Bible. I, having decided that it does not matter much what kind of fins you wear as they all work well, write up my log. About seven I get cook to make me some more tea, and shortly after find myself confronted with difficulties as to the disposal of the two mission teachers for the night. This class of man has no resource in him, and I think worse of the effects of mission-teaching than usual as I prepare to try and get a sleep; not an elaborate affair, I assure you, for I only want to wrap myself round in a blanket and lie on that plank, but the rain has got into the blankets and horror! there is no pillow. The mission men have cleared their bed paraphernalia right out. Now you can do without a good many things, but not without a pillow, so hunt round to find something to make one with; find the Bible in English, the Bible in German, and two hymn-books, and a candle-stick. These seem all the small articles in the room—no, there is a parcel behind the books—mission teachers' Sunday trousers—make delightful arrangement of books bound round with trousers and the whole affair wrapped in one of my towels. Never saw till now advantage of Africans having trousers. Civilisation has its points after all. But it is no use trying to get any sleep until those men are quieter. The partition which separates my apartment from theirs is a bamboo and mat affair, straight at the top so leaving under the roof a triangular space above common to both rooms. Also common to both rooms are the smoke of the fire and the conversation. Kefalla is holding forth in a dogmatic way, and some of the others are snoring. There is a new idea in decoration along the separating wall. Mr. Morris might have made something out of it for a dado. It is composed of an arrangement in line of stretched out singlets. Vaseline the revolver. Wish those men would leave off chattering. Kefalla seems to know the worst about most of the people, black and white, down in Ambas Bay, but I do not believe those last two stories. Evidently great jokes in next room now; Kefalla has thrown himself, still talking, in the dark, on to the top of one of the mission teachers. The women of the village outside have been keeping up, this hour and more, a most melancholy coo-ōoing. Those foolish creatures are evidently worrying about their husbands who have gone down to market in Ambas Bay, and who, they think, are lost in the bush. I have not a shadow of a doubt that those husbands who are not home by now are safely drunk in town, or reposing on the grand new road the kindly Government have provided for them, either in one of the side drains, or tucked in among the lava rock.

QUESTIONS

1. How is the colonial government constructing the "unfinished road"?
2. What is the ecological environment through which Kingsley travels?
3. Is Kingsley's experience shaped by her gender? How?
4. What does the conflict between the "Senegal men" and the "Kruboys" suggest about national and colonial identities in late nineteenth century Africa?

from THINGS FALL APART

Chinua Achebe

Chinua Achebe was born in the Ibgo region of southwestern Nigeria in 1930, the son of a teacher in a missionary school. After receiving his primary and secondary education in Nigeria, he finished a B.A. from the University of London in 1953. He returned to West Africa, working briefly as a teacher and later as the director of a radio station. During this period, he began writing novels, of which Things Fall Apart *was the first. Achebe subsequently became a university professor, teaching at institutions in Africa, Europe, and the United States.*

Things Fall Apart *was published in 1958 and has become among the most widely read of all African novels. In it, Achebe examines the dynamic nature of pre-colonial Igbo society and the challenges that society faces on encountering Europeans. Written during the period of decolonization in West Africa, the novel looks back at the moment of colonization with a view to finding a redeemable past.*

CHAPTER ONE

Okonkwo was well known throughout the nine villages and even beyond. His fame rested on solid personal achievements. As a young man of eighteen he had brought honour to his village by throwing Amalinze the Cat. Amalinze was the great wrestler who for seven years was unbeaten, from Umuofia to Mbaino. He was called the Cat because his back would never touch the earth. It was this man that Okonkwo threw in a fight which the old men agreed was one of the fiercest since the founder of their town engaged a spirit of the wild for seven days and seven nights.

The drums beat and the flutes sang and the spectators held their breath. Amalinze was a wily craftsman, but Okonkwo was as slippery as a fish in water. Every nerve and every muscle stood out on their arms, on their backs and their thighs, and one almost heard them stretching to breaking point. In the end Okonkwo threw the Cat.

That was many years ago, twenty years or more, and during this time Okonkwo's fame had grown like a bush-fire in the harmattan. He was tall and huge, and his bushy eyebrows and wide nose gave him a very severe look. He breathed heavily, and it was said that, when he slept, his wives and children in their out-houses could hear him breathe. When he walked, his heels hardly touched the ground and he seemed to walk on springs, as if he was going to pounce on somebody. And he did pounce on people quite often. He had a slight stammer and whenever he was angry and could not get his words out quickly enough, he would use his fists. He had no patience with unsuccessful men. He had had no patience with his father.

Unoka, for that was his father's name, had died ten years ago. In his day he was lazy and improvident and was quite incapable of thinking about tomorrow. If any money came his way, and it seldom did, he immediately bought gourds of palm-wine, called round his neighbours and made merry. He always said that whenever he saw a dead man's mouth he saw the folly of not eating what one had in one's lifetime. Unoka was, of course, a debtor, and he owed every neighbour some money, from a few cowries to quite substantial amounts.

He was tall but very thin and had a slight stoop. He wore a haggard and mournful look except when he was drinking or playing on his flute. He was very good on his flute, and his happiest moments were the two or three moons after the harvest when the village musicians brought down their instruments, hung above the fireplace. Unoka would play with them, his face beaming with blessedness and peace. Sometimes another village would ask Unoka's band and their dancing *egwugwu* to come and stay with them and teach them their tunes. They would go to such hosts for as long as three or four markets, making music and feasting. Unoka loved the good fare and the good fellowship, and he loved this season of the year, when the rains had stopped and the sun rose every morning with dazzling beauty. And it was not too hot either, because the cold and dry harmattan wind was blowing down from the north. Some years the harmattan was very severe and a dense haze hung on the atmosphere. Old men and children would then sit round log fires, warming their bodies. Unoka loved it all, and he loved the first kites that returned with the dry season, and the children who sang songs of welcome to them. He would remember his own childhood, how he had often wandered around looking for a kite sailing leisurely against the blue sky. As soon as he found one he would sing with his whole being, welcoming it back from its long, long journey, and asking it if it had brought home any lengths of cloth.

That was years ago, when he was young. Unoka, the grown-up, was a failure. He was poor and his wife and children had barely enough to eat. People laughed at him because he was a loafer, and they swore never to lend him any more money because he never paid back. But Unoka was such a man that he always succeeded in borrowing more, and piling up his debts.

One day a neighbour called Okoye came in to see him. He was reclining on a mud bed in his hut playing on the flute. He immediately rose and shook hands with Okoye, who then unrolled the goatskin which he carried under his arm, and sat down. Unoka went into an inner room and soon returned with a small wooden disc containing a kola nut, some alligator pepper and a lump of white chalk.

'I have kola,' he announced when he sat down, and passed the disc over to his guest.

'Thank you. He who brings kola brings life. But I think you ought to break it,' replied Okoye passing back the disc.

'No, it is for you, I think,' and they argued like this for a few moments before Unoka accepted the honour of breaking the kola. Okoye, meanwhile, took the lump of chalk, drew some lines on the floor, and then painted his big toe. As he broke the kola, Unoka prayed to their ancestors for life and health, and for protection against their enemies. When they had eaten they talked about many things: about the heavy rains which were drowning the yams, about the next ancestral feast and about the impending war with the village of Mbaino. Unoka was never happy when it came to wars. He was in fact a coward and could not bear the sight of blood. And so he changed the subject and talked about music, and his face beamed. He could hear in his mind's ear the blood-stirring and intricate rhythms of the *ekwe* and the *udu* and the *ogene*, and he could hear his own flute weaving in and out of them, decorating them with a colourful and plaintive tune. The total effect was gay and brisk, but if one picked out the flute as it went up and down and then broke up into short snatches, one saw that there was sorrow and grief there.

Okoye was also a musician. He played on the *ogene*. But he was not a failure like Unoka. He had a large barn full of yams and he had three wives. And now he was going to take the Idemili title, the third highest in the land. It was a very expensive ceremony and he was gathering all his resources together. That was in fact the reason why he had come to see Unoka. He cleared his throat and began:

'Thank you for the kola. You may have heard of the title I intend to take shortly.'

Having spoken plainly so far, Okoye said the next half a dozen sentences in proverbs. Among the Ibo the art of conversation is regarded very highly, and proverbs are the palm-oil with which words are eaten. Okoye was a great talker and he spoke for a long time, skirting round the subject and then hitting it finally. In short, he was asking Unoka to return the two hundred cowries he had borrowed from him more than two years before. As soon as Unoka understood what his friend was driving at, he burst out laughing. He laughed loud and long and his voice rang out clear as the *ogene*, and tears stood in his eyes. His visitor was amazed, and sat speechless. At the end, Unoka was able to give an answer between fresh outbursts of mirth.

'Look at that wall,' he said, pointing at the far wall of his hut, which was rubbed with red earth so that it shone. 'Look at those lines of chalk;' and Okoye saw groups of short perpendicular lines drawn in chalk. There were five groups, and the smallest group had ten lines. Unoka had a sense of the dramatic and so he allowed a pause, in which he took a pinch of snuff and sneezed noisily, and then he continued: 'Each group there represents a debt to someone, and each stroke is one hundred cowries. You see, I owe that man a thousand cowries. But he has not come to wake me up in the morning for it. I shall pay you, but not today. Our elders say that the sun will shine on those who stand before it shines on those who kneel under them. I shall pay my big debts first.' And he took another pinch of snuff, as if that was paying the big debts first. Okoye rolled his goatskin and departed.

When Unoka died he had taken no title at all and he was heavily in debt. Any wonder then that his son Okonkwo was ashamed of him? Fortunately, among these people a man was judged according to his worth and not according to the worth of his father. Okonkwo was clearly cut out for great things. He was still young but he had won fame as the greatest wrestler in the nine villages. He was a wealthy farmer and had two barns full of yams, and had just married his third wife. To crown it all he had taken two titles and had shown incredible prowess in two inter-tribal wars. And so although Okonkwo was still young, he was already one of the greatest men of his time. Age was respected among his people, but achievement was revered. As the elders said, if a child washed his hands he could eat with kings. Okonkwo had clearly washed his hands and so he ate with kings and elders. And that was how he came to look after the doomed lad who was sacrificed to the village of Umuofia by their neigh-bours to avoid war and bloodshed. The ill-fated lad was called Ikemefuna.

QUESTIONS

1. Why is Okonkwo ashamed of his father?
2. What is the harmattan and how does it affect life in the village?
3. What does the general opinion of Unoka indicate about Igbo ideas of masculinity?
4. Who seems to be Achebe's intended audience for his novel?

METHODS OF NATIVE ADMINISTRATION: POLITICAL OFFICERS AND NATIVE RULERS

Lord Frederick Lugard

Lord Frederick Lugard was born in India in 1858, the son of Rev. F. G. Lugard. After being educated at the Royal Military College, he entered the army. He was assigned to a number of imperial outposts, including Afghanistan, Burma, and Uganda. Lugard became High Commissioner of Northern Nigeria in 1900. Over the next six years, he developed the concept of Indirect Rule, a strategy whereby the British ruled through existing, traditional authorities. Lugard later became Governor of Nigeria and attempted to implement his policies throughout the country. Indirect Rule became accepted as a technique of rule throughout the British Empire during the 1920s and 30s.

Lugard's instructions to political officers elaborates on the details of Indirect Rule. In "Methods of Native Administration: Political Officers and Native Rulers," he emphasizes that the goal of his policies is to bring "civilization" to Africans without interfering in existing social structures. This paradoxical goal, he writes, is to be accomplished through political officers who understand native customs and are able to balance the concerns of the colonized with the best interests of the Empire.

Reprinted from *Instructions to Political and Other Officers, on Subjects Chiefly Political and Administrative,* 1906.

The object in view. The British role here is to bring to the country all the gains of civilisation by applied science (whether in the development of material resources, or the eradication of disease, &c.), with as little interference as possible with Native customs and modes of thought. Where new ideas are to be presented to the native mind, patient explanation of the objects in view will be well rewarded, and new methods may often be clothed in a familiar garb. . . .

Connotation of names of ranks. The term "Resident" implies duties rather of a Political or advisory nature, while the term "Commissioner" connotes functions of a more directly Administrative character. The former is therefore applicable to the Chief Government Officer in a Province of which large areas are under the immediate rule of a Paramount Chief, who, with Native Officials, himself administers a form of Government. The latter is more adapted to Provinces, or parts of Provinces, less advanced in civilisation, where the authority of the Native Chiefs is small, and a large measure of direct Administration must devolve upon the Protectorate Government. The term "Commissioner" is, however, already used in so many other connections, viz., a Commissioner of the Supreme or Provincial Court,—a member of a Commission of Inquiry, a Police Commissioner, &c., that for the sake both of distinction and of brevity, the term Resident has been adopted to denote the two highest grades in the Administrative or Political Department, and the term District Officer though strictly applicable only to the next two grades will be used in this Memorandum to include an Assistant District Officer.

General nature of Administrative Officer's duties. It is the duty of Residents to carry out loyally the policy of the Governor, and not to inaugurate policies of their own. The Governor, through the Lieutenant-Governor, is at all time ready and anxious to hear, and to give full and careful consideration to the views of Residents, but, when once a decision has been arrived at, he expects Residents to give effect to it in a thorough and loyal spirit, and to inculcate the same spirit in their juniors. This does not mean a rigid adherence to the letter of a ruling. Among such diverse races in widely varying degrees of advancement, it is inevitable and desirable that there should be diversity in the application of a general policy by the Resident, who knows the local conditions and feelings of his people. It does mean, however, that the principles underlying the policy are to be observed and the Resident in modifying their application will fully inform and obtain the approval of the Governor.

Festina lente ["Make haste slowly," *ed.*] is a motto very applicable to Africa, provided that the coach is not set on the wrong rail, so that a wrong course—temporarily easy—is inaugurated. By shirking initial difficulties and yielding to prejudice far greater difficulties must be encountered later. . . .

The Government relies on its Administrative Officers to keep in close touch with Native opinion and feeling, and to report for the information of the Governor. It is thus only that we can produce the best results,—that the Governor and Lieutenant-Governors can keep in touch and gain information, and the Political Officer can count on support and on recognition of his work.

Difference of method in advanced or backward Communities:—

(a) *Advanced tribes.* The degree to which a Political Officer may be called upon to act in an administrative capacity, will thus depend upon the influence and ability of the Native Chiefs in each part of the Province, though in every case he will endeavour to rule through the Native Chiefs.

In those parts of Provinces which are under the immediate authority of a Chief of the first or of the second grade, the primary duty and object of a Political Officer will be to educate them in the duties of Rulers according to a civilised standard; to convince them that oppression of the people is not sound policy, or to the eventual benefit of the rulers; to bring home to their intelligence, as far as may be, the evils attendant on a system which holds the lower classes in a state of slavery or serfdom, and so destroys individual responsibility, ambition, and development amongst them; to impress upon them the advantage of delegating the control of districts to subordinate Chiefs, and of trusting and encouraging these subordinates, while keeping a strict supervision over them; to see that there is no favouritism in such appointments; and to inculcate the unspeakable benefit of justice, free from bribery and open to all.

Where taxation exists the consequent duty of assessing all the towns and villages himself will throw upon the Political Officer a considerable amount of purely Administrative work, even in such districts. In this work he should invite the co-operation of the Chief, and endeavour to enlist his cordial assistance by making it clear to him that his own interests are deeply involved.

(b) *Backward tribes*. In districts where there is no Chief of the first or second grade, a Political Officer's functions become more largely Administrative, and among uncivilised Pagan tribes he must assume the full onus of Administration, to the extent to which time and opportunity permit. In such communities he will constantly endeavour to support the authority of the Chief, and encourage him to show initiative. If there is no Chief who exercises authority beyond his own village, he will encourage any village Chief of influence and character to control a group of villages, with a view to making him Chief of a district later if he shows ability for the charge. Native Court clerks or scribes, constables or couriers will never be allowed to usurp the authority of the Native Chief or Village Head. . . .

Position and duties of Resident in charge. The Resident is the senior Government Official in the Province, and represents the Lieutenant-Governor in all Administrative matters. In the absence of a responsible officer of any Department it is his duty to report any dereliction of duty on the part of any departmental subordinate to the Head of his Department, or if of a serious nature to the Lieutenant-Governor. All such officers will be guided by the instructions and wishes of the Resident, so far as they are not incompatible with the orders they have received from the head of their department, to whom they will report the matter if the Resident's instructions conflict with departmental orders. The Head of a Department issues his instructions direct to his subordinate officer, and it is the duty of the subordinate to keep the Resident fully informed of any orders he receives which it may be useful for him to know, as, for instance, a Public Works Department Officer who had received orders to commence the repair of houses, &c. If the subordinate is a Native clerk the District Officer will be regarded as the local representative, and communications from the Head of the Department will be addressed to him. . . .

The first and most essential duties of a Resident and his staff are those in connection with the conduct of Native Administration, including the close supervision of the Native Courts and the assessment for taxation. This work is sufficiently onerous, and it cannot be adequately performed if a Resident is charged in addition with work and correspondence of a general administrative nature. As the senior representative of Government in his province, he cannot be entirely relieved of all general administrative duties, but in the scheme of administration in Nigeria for which I am responsible, it has been my endeavour to relieve him of them as far as possible (*a*) by the creation of Lieutenant-Governors with an adequate Secretariat to undertake it, and (*b*) by the appointment of Station Magistrates charged with the Police Court work at large centres, and with the conduct of non-political questions and correspondence.

Junior Staff. Residents will spare no efforts to instruct young Officers posted to their Staff, and will see that all are familiar with the Ordinances, Regulations, General Orders, and Political Memos. These constitute the "laws and usages" of the Protectorate, which all Political Officers are bound by their oath to enforce impartially. District Officers in charge of Divisions will send full reports to the Resident, from which he will extract any information useful for his half-yearly and Annual Report to the Lieutenant-Governor, to whom he will forward all assessment reports and any particular report, or quote paragraphs from it, if of particular interest, so as to afford the Lieutenant-Governor an opportunity of gauging the abilities of Junior Officers. Assistant District Officers will submit their reports to or through their Divisional Officer, as the Resident may direct. Junior Officers will not be employed at Headquarters on clerical or accounting work which the Native Staff is capable of performing. District Officers will reside at the administrative centre of the division to which they are posted, and remain responsible to the Province. Whenever there are any Assistant District Officers in excess of the establishment, they will be temporarily posted to the Secretariat for six months' training.

Necessity for constant traveling. Political Officers must endeavour to preserve a proper equilibrium between their Judicial and Executive duties, neither allowing the former to engross all their time and to detain them at their Headquarters, nor becoming so absorbed in assessment, and other executive work, as to neglect Judicial duties and leave cases to the Native Courts which would be more advisedly tried by the Provincial Court.

"The work done by a Political Officer," said Sir H. Lawrence, "in his district, surrounded by the people, is greatly superior to the work done in office surrounded by untrustworthy officials." A District Officer should pass from place to place and endeavour to lessen oppression and bribery, and to watch over and improve the Native tribunals. He should when possible be accompanied by the local Chief or district Head. He will of course at the same time hold his Court wherever he may be, and take opportunity to do so in a formal manner in the principal towns.

The primary object of travelling through the Province is, that the Political Officer may show himself to the people and hear their complaints at first hand, not trusting to the reports which reach him at Headquarters, where the villagers may possibly often fear to carry complaints, especially if they refer to some petty oppression or illegal exaction by the Chiefs. It is only by the advent of a British Officer that scoundrels, misrepresenting the complaints, troubles and what they will from the Natives in the name of Government, can be caught; for the villagers in their ignorance, supposing them to be genuine, dare not as a rule complain.

It has been abundantly shown by experience that "unrest," resulting in murders and outrages, and eventually necessitating the use of force, inevitably take place among primitive tribes when *districts are not regularly* and systematically *visited*. By frequent touring, abuses are redressed before they become formidable, the law-abiding people are encouraged to restrain the turbulent and lawless elements, and trust and confidence in Government is fostered.

In Provinces where there is direct taxation, officials should be constantly passing from place to place, for the purpose of carrying out the assessment of every village. . . . or verifying and revising the initial assessment. But whether there is direct taxation or not, it is equally the duty of a Political Officer to travel constantly, in order to record, or to add to the statistics required for the Provincial Records; to verify or fix the areas of jurisdiction of each District Headman and Chief, or Native Court; and to become personally acquainted with the various peoples in his district. These duties are of primary importance in the early stage of administration and organisation. . . .

Travelling, it must be remembered, costs money for transport, and is not undertaken for pleasure. Each journey, therefore, should achieve some definite and useful result. . . .

A Veterinary or Forestry Officer, or Public Works Department Officer, or persons involved in building, and any other departmental officer who has occasion to travel in a Province should seize the opportunity of accompanying a Political Officer on tour. It is not, however, essential that a departmental officer should be accompanied by a Political Officer, since such a course would frequently result in mutual delay, but he would generally be accompanied by one of the native political staff to facilitate his work.

Languages. All Officers of the Political Staff are required to pass an examination in the Ordinances and Regulations of Nigeria, in the General Orders, and in one of the chief Native languages of Nigeria. Proficiency in a Native language is an important qualification for promotion. Promotion will ordinarily be provisional only unless an officer has passed, and he will be liable to revert if he does not do so within the period prescribed. Assistant District Officers must pass the Lower Standard to qualify for promotion, and a Resident should have passed the Higher Standard, especially if the language he has adopted is Hausa.

Continuity essential in Africa. I regard continuity of Administration as a matter of paramount and indeed of vital importance in African Administration. It is only after many years of personal contact that the African—naturally reserved and suspicious towards strangers—will give his confidence unreservedly. More can often be accomplished in half-an-hour by an officer well known and trusted by the people, than by another, though his superior in ability, after months of patient effort.

It has, therefore, been my general rule, that the more senior an officer becomes the less liable he is for transfer from his Province. An Assistant District Officer may be posted to two or three Provinces in succession, in order that he may gain experience, and the Lieutenant-Governor may decide whether his abilities are best adapted for work in an advanced, or a backward Province. As a Second Class District Officer he has become more of a fixture, and finally when he becomes Resident in substantive charge of a Province he is never taken away from it.

These rules are of course liable to violation owing to sudden vacancies, &c., more especially of late under war conditions, but though a Senior Officer may be removed for a time he will be restored to the Province he knows and to the people who know and trust him as soon as circumstances permit. Now that there is a single Administrative roster for all Nigeria, a Southern Provinces Officer may find himself posted on promotion to the Northern Provinces and *vice versa.* But here again the change will not as a rule be permanent, especially amongst the Senior Officers, and I should endeavour to restore an Officer to the people whose language he has learnt, and among whom he can do more efficient work, as soon as an exchange could be effected. Residents in like manner will avoid changing their Staff from one division to another if it can be helped.

Relations of the Political Officers with Resident and Native Administration. The Political Officer is the channel of communication between all Departmental Officers and the Native Administration. It is essential that a Resident shall be fully informed of any project which a Departmental Officer proposes to inaugurate, and he will inform the Emir and enlist his assistance. If after consulting the Emir he considers that the project—or the manner in which it is proposed to carry it out—is inadvisable he will refer to the Lieutenant-Governor, and it will be held in abeyance until a reply is received. The general scope of the work having thus been discussed and approved, the Departmental Officer is at liberty to give orders as to details, but if he desires to introduce any new principle he will again consult the Resident. If the work is to be carried out at some distance from the Capital, a responsible Native official will usually be attached to the Departmental Officer, through whom he can make his requisitions for labour, &c., and issue his instructions. If the matter is urgent, and the Departmental Officer finds it necessary to issue instructions without delay, he will fully inform the Resident, in order that he in turn may inform the Native Administration.

While these instructions are of especial importance where the expenditure of Native Administration funds is involved, the general principle will also be observed in the execution of duties or works which are paid for from departmental votes. In the former case the Native Administration has the right to determine the priority in which different works shall be carried out, and the method subject to any technical objections. Thus, when subject to the approval of the Governor the Native Administration provides funds for the construction of several different sections of roads, the construction of which is placed in the hands of the Public Works Department, it is admissible that the Native Administration should decide which road should take priority, and if it is itself capable of carrying out the earthworks, it may request the Public Works Department to deal with the alignment, bridges, and culverts, and only to exercise a general supervision over the remainder. Since, however, the road may eventually become a metalled motor track under the Public Works Department charge, it is clear that the construction must be in accordance with technical instructions. On the other hand a Departmental Officer carrying out Government work from Departmental votes—such as the repair of telegraphs—will look to the District Officer to assist him in procuring the necessary labour and supplies, usually, as I have said, through the medium of an official of the Native Administration. Departmental Officers must bear in mind that, in order to obtain the full benefit of Native co-operation, the orders must be given not by the Resident or any of his Staff, but by the Head Chief. . . .

Where the duties of a Departmental Officer are educational, *e.g.,* Medical and Sanitary, Forestry, Agriculture, and Veterinary—and he is engaged on a tour of instruction, it is desirable that he should inform the Resident of the nature of the advice he proposes to give, especially if it involves a specific course of action, in order that the Resident may instruct his Staff and the Native Administration of that course of action, and also in order that there may be no conflict of instructions. I recollect an instance in which two Departmental Officers, visiting the same town within a short time of each other, each with a different object in view gave diametrically opposite instructions on a specific point to the local Chief. In such a case the Resident would have been able to discuss the matter with both and to arrive at a clear course of action. Political Officers are, moreover, able to put a Departmental Officer in possession of local conditions and prejudices, and so to assist him in his objects. . . .

Judicial functions. The Resident in charge of a Province has *ex-officio* full powers as Judge of the Provincial Court of the Province, of which his European Staff are "Commissioners." The Judicial powers of a Commissioner may be increased at the discretion of the Lieutenant-Governor, irrespective of his rank, on the recommendation of the Resident and of the Legal Adviser, in accordance with the ability he shows in his judicial work. Evidence of judicial ability will necessarily count much in selection for promotion. . . .

Native Courts. A Resident will establish a Native Court in every city or district where it appears advisable to do so, and will constantly supervise its work, especially in the lower grades of Courts. He must of course carefully study the Native Courts Ordinance and Memo. 8. In Courts of Grades A and B he will watch the integrity of the Native Judges, and note their comparative ability for promotion to more important centres, and see that their sentences are in accord with British conceptions of humanity. In the lower grades he will take care that the initiative of the Chiefs who compose the Court is not interfered with by the clerk or scribe, that they do not exceed their powers, and that their sentences and findings are free from bias.

The "Province," "Division," and "District." A Province is a single entity under the control of the Resident in charge. It is divided into "Divisions" under District Officers responsible to the Resident. The Divisions must not be confused with the "districts" under Native Headmen. The more important divisions will be under first-class, and the less important under second-class District Officers. The charge of a first or second-class division is an appointment notified in the Gazette, which forms the Treasurer's authority to disburse the duty pay which attaches to it.

The division in which the Headquarters of the Province is situated will usually be in charge of a District Officer, like any other division, so far as its routine work is concerned, but it is, I think, of great importance that in the more advanced Provinces the paramount Chief should deal direct with the Resident, and he is apt to feel slighted if referred to a subordinate Officer. He should not only have free access to the Resident at all times, but should not be debarred from consulting him in any matter, even of detail, regarding the "Emirate Division" even though the matter may eventually and properly be dealt with by the District Officer. In Provinces where there is no paramount Chief and only an embryonic Native Administration, the Resident will generally be able to take charge of the Headquarter division himself with the assistance of a District Officer who can take his place when on tour.

The number of divisions in a Province is subject to the approval of the Governor, and they will be notified in the Gazette, but their boundaries may at any time be altered by the Lieutenant-Governor subject to the stipulations in this paragraph. One or more Assistant District Officers will be attached to each division, either generally or to a particular district, as the Resident may decide. Each Divisional Officer will tour constantly in his division hearing complaints, recording statistics, inspecting Native Courts, checking native agents, surveying, and assessing, and supervising the collection of taxes where these are imposed. He will reside near the principal town of the division, and each division in turn will be visited by the Resident. The Divisional Headquarters (involving the erection of new buildings, as well as political considerations) will not be transferred to another place without the prior concurrence of the Governor. The Resident himself will reside at the Provincial capital, which will also usually be the Headquarters of the Military detachment (if any) and of the Medical and Police Officers. Wherever he wishes to go on tour the District Officer in charge of the Headquarter division will deal with any urgent correspondence addressed to him or any urgent matter as may be directed by the Resident, unless the "relief Resident" is present. . . .

A Province, or even a Division, may comprise various units of Native Administration, but in no case will such a unit be comprised partly in one Province and partly in another; and the same applies as a rule to a Division. The limits of the jurisdiction and authority of Native Chiefs may not be altered, or one Emirate or Chieftainship placed under another, without the sanction of the Lieutenant-Governor, who will in any case of importance consult the Governor. Such reference is necessary when it is proposed to subordinate a Chief hitherto independent, and more especially an independent Pagan Community to a Moslem Emirate—which should very rarely, if ever, be done.

Departmental functions of Political Officers. A Political Officer has to represent various Departments and to exercise divers functions in the Province to which he belongs. He acts as *Postal Officer*, in the absence of an European Officer of the Department, and is responsible for the despatch of mails in transit, and for the various duties laid down in the Regulations under the Postal Ordinance. The Postal and Telegraph Clerks, under his general supervision, will undertake the duties of issuing stamps, and preparing receipts for parcels and registered letters, &c.

The *Police* in his Province are under the general orders of the Resident, whose relation to them and to the Commissioner or Assistant Commissioner of Police is laid down in Police Regulations and in General Orders and elsewhere. Isolated Police Constables should never be stationed in villages since it deprives the Village Headman of responsibility and initiative; and men placed in such a position of power are apt to misuse their authority. Detachments without a European are always to be deprecated. When in charge of the Government prison, the District Officer will inspect it frequently and check the prisoners with the warrants at least once a month.

Political Officers will also assist the *Customs* on those inland frontiers where it is not possible for the Department to have an European representative, and also in the collection of Customs dues on Postal parcels; and in such capacity they exercise the powers of Customs Officers, and any preventive staff is under their orders. . . .

QUESTIONS

1. What are the responsibilities of a "Resident"?
2. What language requirements are expected of Political Officers?
3. How do Lugard's definitions of civilization and progress reflect the assumptions of the period in which he lived?
4. What do Lugard's instructions suggest about the extent and nature of British imperial bureaucracy?

World War I

STORM OF STEEL

Ernst Jünger

Ernst Jünger (1895–1998) left his middle-class German home in 1912 in search of adventure. Military life attracted him, so he enlisted in the renowned French Foreign Legion. On the outbreak of World War I, he returned to Germany, where at the age of nineteen he enlisted in the forces and became a lieutenant on the western front. Jünger served in the trenches throughout the war and received a medal for bravery. Afterward, he studied philosophy and natural science. When Jünger first began to write, his work brought him to the attention of the newly formed Nazi party, but he did not join and did not support many of the Nazi causes. He enlisted again in World War II and was one of the officers involved in the abortive attempt on Hitler's life in 1944. After the war, Jünger's militarist attitudes changed radically, and he became an active campaigner for peace and European unity.

Storm of Steel (1920) was Jünger's first novel. A memoir of his days in the trenches, it graphically portrays the lives of the soldiers—both the privations they suffered, and the bonds among them.

THE AUTHOR'S PREFACE

I was a nineteen-year-old lieutenant in command of a platoon, and my part of the line was easily recognizable from the English side by a row of tall shell-stripped trees that rose from the ruins of Monchy. My left flank was bounded by the sunken road leading to Berles-au-Bois, which was in the hands of the English; my right was marked by a sap running out from our lines, one that helped us many a time to make our presence felt by means of bombs and rifle grenades.

Today there is no secret about what those trenches concealed, and a book such as this may, like a trench map years after the event, be read with sympathy and interest by the other side. But here not only the blue and red lines of the trenches are shown, but the blood that beat and the life that lay hid in them.

Time only strengthens my conviction that it was a good and strenuous life, and that the war, for all its destructiveness, was an incomparable schooling of the heart. The front-line soldier whose foot came down on the earth so grimly and harshly may claim this at least, that it came down cleanly. Warlike achievements are enhanced by the inherent worth of the enemy.

On the 23d of August we were transported in lorries to Le Mesnil. Our spirits were excellent, though we knew we were going to be put in where the battle of Somme was at its worst. Chaff and laughter went from lorry to lorry. We marched from Le Mesnil at dusk to Sailly-Saillisel, and here the battalion dumped packs in a large meadow and paraded in battle order.

Artillery fire of a hitherto unimagined intensity rolled and thundered on our front. Thousands of twitching flashes turned the western horizon into a sea of flowers. All the while the wounded came trailing back with white, dejected faces, huddled into the ditches by the gun and ammunition columns that rattled past.

A man in a steel helmet reported to me as guide to conduct my platoon to the renowned Combles, where for the time we were to be in reserve. Sitting with him at the side of the road, I asked him, naturally enough, what it was like in the line. In reply I heard a monotonous tale of crouching all day in shell holes with no one on either flank and no trenches communicating with the rear, of unceasing attacks, of dead bodies littering the ground, of maddening thirst, of wounded and dying, and of a lot besides. The face half-framed by the steel rim of the helmet was unmoved; the voice accompanied by the sound of battle droned on, and the impression they made on me was one of unearthly solemnity. One could see that the man had been through horror to the limit of despair and there had learned to despise it. Nothing was left but supreme and superhuman indifference.

JÜNGER: STORM OF STEEL

"Where you fall, there you lie. No one can help you. No one knows whether he will come back alive. They attack every day, but they can't get through. Everybody knows it is life and death."

As far as we could see in the darkness, Combles was utterly shot to bits. The damage seemed to be recent, judging from the amount of timber among the ruins and the contents of the houses slung over the road. We climbed over numerous heaps of débris—rather hurriedly, owing to a few shrapnel shells—and reached our quarters. They were in a large, shot-riddled house. Here I established myself with three sections. The other two occupied the cellar of a ruin opposite.

At 4 a.m. we were aroused from our rest on the fragments of bed we had collected, in order to receive steel helmets. It was also the occasion of discovering a sack of coffee beans in a corner of the cellar; whereupon there followed a great brewing of coffee.

After breakfast I went out to have a look round. Heavy artillery had turned a peaceful little billeting town into a scene of desolation in the course of a day or two. Whole houses had been flattened by single direct hits or blown up so that the interiors of the rooms hung over the chaos like the scenes on a stage. A sickly scent of dead bodies rose from many of the ruins, for many civilians had been caught in the bombardment and buried beneath the wreckage of their homes. A little girl lay dead in a pool of blood on the threshold of one of the doorways.

The square in front of the ruins of the church had been particularly hard hit. Here was the entrance to the catacombs, a very ancient underground passage with recesses here and there in which were crowded the staffs of all the units engaged. It was said that the civilians had opened up the entrance with pickaxes when the bombardment began. It had been walled up and kept secret from the Germans during the whole of their occupation. The streets were reduced to narrow paths winding circuitously round and over heaps of timber and masonry. Quantities of fruit and vegetables were going to waste in the churned-up gardens.

A plentiful supply of "iron rations" provided us with a dinner that we cooked in the kitchen, and concluded, needless to say, with strong coffee. I then settled myself in an armchair upstairs. From letters scattered about I saw that the house belonged to a brewer, Lesage. Cupboards and chests of drawers were thrown open; there was an overturned washstand, a sewing machine, and a perambulator. The pictures and the looking glasses on the walls were all broken. Drawers had been pulled out and emptied, and a yard deep all over the floor were underclothes, corsets, books, papers, bedroom tables, broken glass, bottles, notebooks, chair legs, coats, cloaks, lamps, curtains, window frames, doors torn from their hinges, lace, photographs, oil paintings, albums, broken boxes, hats, flower pots, and torn wall paper, all tangled up together in wild confusion.

In the course of the afternoon the firing increased to such a degree that single explosions were no longer audible. There was nothing but one terrific tornado of noise. From seven onward the square and the houses round were shelled at intervals of half a minute with fifteen-centimeter shells. There were many duds among them, which all the same made the houses rock. We sat all this while in our cellar, round a table, on armchairs covered in silk, with our heads propped on our hands, and counted the seconds between the explosions. Our jests became less frequent, till at last the foolhardiest of us fell silent, and at eight o'clock two direct hits brought down the next house.

From nine to ten the shelling was frantic. The earth rocked and the sky boiled like a gigantic cauldron.

Hundreds of heavy batteries were concentrated on and round Combles. Innumerable shells came howling and hurtling over us. Thick smoke, ominously lit up by Very lights, veiled everything. Head and ears ached violently, and we could only make ourselves understood by shouting a word at a time. The power of logical thought and the force of gravity seemed alike to be suspended. One had the sense of something as unescapable and as unconditionally fated as a catastrophe of nature. An N.C.O. of No. 3 platoon went mad.

At ten this carnival of hell gradually calmed down and passed into a steady drum fire. It was still certainly impossible to distinguish one shell from another.

At last we reached the front line. It was held by men cowering close in the shell holes, and their dead voices trembled with joy when they heard that we were the relief. A Bavarian sergeant major briefly handed over the sector and the Very-light pistol.

My platoon formed the right wing of the position held by the regiment. It consisted of a shallow sunken road which had been pounded by shells. It was a few hundred meters left of Guillemont and a rather shorter distance right of Bois-de-Trônes. We were parted from the troops on our right, the Seventy-sixth Regiment of Infantry, by a space about five hundred meters wide. This space was shelled so violently that no troops could maintain themselves there.

As I had no idea how far off the enemy were, I warned my men to be ready for the worst. We all remained on guard. I spent the night with my batman and two orderlies in a hole perhaps one yard square and one yard deep.

When day dawned we were astonished to see, by degrees, what a sight surrounded us.

The sunken road now appeared as nothing but a series of enormous shell holes filled with pieces of uniform, weapons, and dead bodies. The ground all round, as far as the eye could see, was plowed by shells. You could search in vain for one wretched blade of grass. This churned-up battlefield was ghastly. Among the living lay the dead. As we dug ourselves in we found them in layers stacked one upon the top of another. One company after another had been shoved into the drum fire and steadily annihilated. The corpses were covered with the masses of soil turned up by the shells, and the next company advanced in the place of the fallen.

The sunken road and the ground behind were full of German dead; the ground in front, of English. Arms, legs, and heads stuck out stark above the lips of the craters. In front of our miserable defenses there were torn-off limbs and corpses over many of which cloaks and ground sheets had been thrown to hide the fixed stare of their distorted features. In spite of the heat no one thought for a moment of covering them with soil.

The village of Guillemont was distinguished from the landscape around it only because the shell holes there were of a whiter color by reason of the houses which had been ground to powder. Guillemont railway station lay in front of us. It was smashed to bits like a child's plaything. Delville Wood, reduced to matchwood, was farther behind.

Day had scarcely dawned when an English flying man descended on us in a steep spin and circled round incessantly like a bird of prey, while we made for our holes and cowered there. Nevertheless, the observer's sharp eyes must have spied us out, for a siren sounded its deep, long-drawn notes above us at short intervals. After a little while it appeared that a battery had received the signal. One heavy shell after another came at us on a flat trajectory with incredible fury. We crouched in our refuges and could do nothing. Now and then we lit a cigar and threw it away again. Every moment we expected a rush of earth to bury us. The sleeve of Schmidt's coat was torn by a big splinter.

At three in the afternoon the men came in from the left flank and said they could stick it no longer, as their shelters were shot to bits. It cost me all my callousness to get them back to their posts.

Just before ten at night the left flank of the regimental front was heavily shelled, and after twenty minutes we came in for it too. In a brief space we were completely covered in dust and smoke, and yet most of the hits were just in front or just behind. While this hurricane was raging I went along my platoon front. The men were standing, rifle in hand, as though carved in stone, their eyes fixed on the ground in front of them. Now and then by the light of a rocket I saw the gleam of helmet after helmet, bayonet after bayonet, and I was filled with pride at commanding this handful of men that might very likely be pounded into the earth but could not be conquered. It is in such moments that the human spirit triumphs over the mightiest demonstrations of material force. The fragile body, steeled by the will, stands up to the most terrific punishment.

QUESTIONS

1. When he wrote *Storm of Steel* Jünger believed that his experience had been a positive one. Why might this be?
2. What was the average soldier's experience in the trenches?
3. How did the war affect those caught up in it?
4. Judging from Jünger's account, why was World War I so devastating? How was it different?
5. Is this an anti-war novel?

Decolonization

DOCUMENT

CONTINENTAL GOVERNMENT
FOR AFRICA

Kwame Nkrumah

Kwame Nkrumah was born in the British colony of the Gold Coast (now Ghana) in 1909. As a young man he traveled to the United States and to Great Britain to pursue his education, and during this time he came in contact with the ideas of early Pan-Africanist Marcus Garvey. In 1945, Nkrumah and George Padmore organized the fifth Pan-Africanist Conference in Manchester, England. After the conference, Nkrumah became increasingly involved in anti-imperial politics and in agitation for African political freedom. He arrived back in the Gold Coast in 1947 and within two years had established a new political party, the Convention People's Party (CPP). Nkrumah was involved in protests and civil disobedience against the British colonial government. He was imprisoned for this, but his actions also helped to convince the British that their hold on the Gold Coast was untenable. In 1951, Nkrumah was released from jail and asked by the British governor to work in cooperation to bring the Gold Coast to independence. He agreed, and when the former colony became the independent state of Ghana in 1957, he was its first president. As head of state, he emphasized the importance of the Organization for African Unity (OAU) and worked to disentangle African economies from colonial ties. At the same time, he became more totalitarian in his policies, and he was ultimately overthrown by a military coup in 1966.

Africa Must Unite constitutes a kind of manifesto of Pan-Africanism. It was published in 1963, at a time when the wave of decolonization had just swept across the continent and optimism ran high. In "Continental Government for

Reprinted by permission from *Africa Must Unite*. Copyright © 1970 by International Publishers.

135

Africa," Nkrumah seeks to learn from the examples set by colonial powers while at the same time extricating Africa from what he sees as the artificial boundaries laid down by colonial occupation.

We have seen, in the example of the United States, how the dynamic elements within society understood the need for unity and fought their bitter civil war to maintain the political union that was threatened by the reactionary forces. We have also seen, in the example of the Soviet Union, how the forging of continental unity along with the retention of national sovereignty by the federal states, has achieved a dynamism that has lifted a most backward society into a most powerful unit within a remarkably short space of time. From the examples before us, in Europe and the United States of America, it is therefore patent that we in Africa have the resources, present and potential, for creating the kind of society that we are anxious to build. It is calculated that by the end of this century the population of Africa will probably exceed five hundred millions.

Our continent gives us the second largest land stretch in the world. The natural wealth of Africa is estimated to be greater than that of almost any other continent in the world. To draw the most from our existing and potential means for the achievement of abundance and a fine social order, we need to unify our efforts, our resources, our skills and intentions.

Europe, by way of contrast, must be a lesson to us all. Too busy hugging its exclusive nationalisms, it has descended, after centuries of wars interspersed with intervals of uneasy peace, into a state of confusion, simply because it failed to build a sound basis of political association and understanding. Only now, under the necessities of economic stringency and the threat of the new German industrial and military rehabilitation, is Europe trying—unsuccessfully—to find a *modus operandi* for containing the threat. It is deceptively hoped that the European Community will perform this miracle. It has taken two world wars and the break-up of empires to press home the lesson, still only partly digested, that strength lies in unity.

While we in Africa, for whom the goal of unity is paramount, are striving to concert our efforts in this direction, the neo-colonialists are straining every nerve to upset them by encouraging the formation of communities based on the languages of their former colonizers. We cannot allow ourselves to be so disorganized and divided. The fact that I speak English does not make me an Englishman. Similarly, the fact that some of us speak French or Portuguese does not make us Frenchmen or Portuguese. We are Africans first and last, and as Africans our best interests can only be served by uniting within an African Community. Neither the Commonwealth nor a Franco-African Community can be a substitute.

To us, Africa with its islands is just one Africa. We reject the idea of any kind of partition. From Tangier or Cairo in the North to Capetown in the South, from Cape Guardafui in the East to Cape Verde Islands in the West, Africa is one and indivisible.

I know that when we speak of political union, our critics are quick to observe an attempt to impose leadership and to abrogate sovereignty. But we have seen from the many examples of union put forward, that equality of the states is jealously guarded in every single constitution and that sovereignty is maintained. There are differences in the powers allotted to the central government and those retained by the states, as well as in the functions of the executive, legislature and judiciary. All of them have a common trade and economic policy. All of them are secular, in order that religion might not be dragged across the many problems involved in maintaining unity and securing the greatest possible development.

We in Africa who are pressing now for unity are deeply conscious of the validity of our purpose. We need the strength of our combined numbers and resources to protect ourselves from the very positive dangers of returning colonialism in disguised forms. We need it to combat the entrenched forces dividing our continent and still holding back millions of our brothers. We need it to secure total African liberation. We need it to carry forward our construction of a socio-economic system that will support the great mass of our steadily rising population at levels of life which will compare with those in the most advanced countries.

But we cannot mobilize our present and potential resources without concerted effort. If we developed our potentialities in men and natural resources in separate isolated groups, our energies would soon be dissipated in the struggle to outbid one another. Economic friction among us would certainly lead to bitter political rivalry, such as for many years hampered the pace of growth and development in Europe.

At present most of the independent African States are moving in directions which expose us to the dangers of imperialism and neo-colonialism. We therefore need a common political basis for the integration of our policies in economic planning, defence, foreign and diplomatic relations. That basis for political action need not infringe the essential sovereignty of the separate African States. These States would continue to exercise independent authority, except in the fields defined and reserved for common action in the interests of the security and orderly development of the whole continent.

In my view, therefore, a united Africa—that is, the political and economic unification of the African Continent—should seek three objectives:

Firstly, we should have an over-all economic planning on a continental basis. This would increase the industrial and economic power of Africa. So long as we remain balkanized, regionally or territorially, we shall be at the mercy of colonialism and imperialism. The lesson of the South American Republics *vis-à-vis* the strength and solidarity of the United States of America is there for all to see.

The resources of Africa can be used to the best advantage and the maximum benefit to all only if they are set within an overall framework of a continentally planned development. An overall economic plan, covering an Africa united on a continental basis, would increase our total industrial and economic power. We should therefore be thinking seriously now of ways and means of building up a Common Market of a United Africa and not allow ourselves to be lured by the dubious advantages of association with the so-called European Common Market. We in Africa have looked outward too long for the development of our economy and transportation. Let us begin to look inwards into the African Continent for all aspects of its development. Our communications were devised under colonial rule to stretch outwards towards Europe and elsewhere, instead of developing internally between our cities and states. Political unity should give us the power and will to change all this. We in Africa have untold agricultural, mineral and water-power resources. These almost fabulous resources can be fully exploited and utilized in the interest of Africa and the African people, only if we develop them within a Union Government of African States. Such a Government will need to maintain a common currency, a monetary zone and a central bank of issue. The advantages of these financial and monetary arrangements would be inestimable, since monetary transactions between our several States would be facilitated and the pace of financial activity generally quickened. A central bank of issue is an inescapable necessity, in view of the need to re-orientate the economy of Africa and place it beyond the reach of foreign control.

Secondly, we should aim at the establishment of a unified military and defence strategy. I do not see much virtue or wisdom in our separate efforts to build up or maintain vast military forces for self-defence which, in any case, would be ineffective in any major attack upon our separate States. If we examine this problem realistically, we should be able to ask ourselves this pertinent question: which single State in Africa today can protect its sovereignty against an imperialist aggressor? In this connec- tion, it should be mentioned that anti-*apartheid* leaders have alleged that South Africa is building a great military force with all the latest weapons of destruction, in order to crush nationalism in Africa. Nor is this all. There are grave indications that certain settler governments in Africa have already been caught in the dangerous arms race and are now arming them- selves to the teeth. Their military activities constitute a serious threat not only to the security of Africa, but also to the peace of the world. If these reports are true, only the unity of Africa can prevent South Africa and these other governments from achieving their diabolical aims.

If we do not unite and combine our military resources for common defence, the individual States, out of a sense of insecurity, may be drawn into making defence pacts with foreign powers which may endanger the security of us all.

There is also the expenditure aspect of this problem. The maintenance of large military forces imposes a heavy financial burden on even the most wealthy States. For young African States, who are in great need of capital for internal development, it is ridiculous—indeed suicidal—for each State separately and individually to assume such a heavy burden of self-defence, when the weight of this burden could be easily lightened by sharing it among themselves. Some attempt has already been made by the Casablanca Powers and the Afro-Malagasy Union in the matter of common defence, but how much better and stronger it would be if, instead of two such ventures, there was one over-all (land, sea and air) Defence Command for Africa.

The third objective which we should have in Africa stems from the first two which I have just described. If we in Africa set up a unified economic

139

planning organization and a unified military and defence strategy, it will be necessary for us to adopt a unified foreign policy and diplomacy to give political direction to our joint efforts for the protection and economic development of our continent. Moreover, there are some sixty odd States in Africa, about thirty-two of which are at present independent. The burden of separate diplomatic representation by each State on the Continent of Africa alone would be crushing, not to mention representation outside Africa. The desirability of a common foreign policy which will enable us to speak with one voice in the councils of the world, is so obvious, vital and imperative that comment is hardly necessary.

I am confident that it should be possible to devise a constitutional structure applicable to our special conditions in Africa and not necessarily framed in terms of the existing constitutions of Europe, America or elsewhere, which will enable us to secure the objectives I have defined and yet preserve to some extent the sovereignty of each State within a Union of African States.

We might erect for the time being a constitutional form that could start with those states willing to create a nucleus, and leave the door open for the attachment of others as they desire to join or reach the freedom which would allow them to do so. The form could be made amenable to adjustment and amendment at any time the consensus of opinion is for it. It may be that concrete expression can be given to our present ideas within a continental parliament that would provide a lower and an upper house, the one to permit the discussion of the many problems facing Africa by a representation based on population; the other, ensuring the equality of the associated States, regardless of size and population, by a similar, limited representation from each of them, to formulate a common policy in all matters affecting the security, defence and development of Africa. It might, through a committee selected for the purpose, examine likely solutions to the problems of union and draft a more conclusive form of constitution that will be acceptable to all the independent States.

The survival of free Africa, the extending independence of this continent, and the development towards that bright future on which our hopes and endeavours are pinned, depend upon political unity.

Under a major political union of Africa there could emerge a United Africa, great and powerful, in which the territorial boundaries which are the relics of colonialism will become obsolete and superfluous, working for the complete and total mobilization of the economic planning organization under a unified political direction. The forces that unite us are far greater than the difficulties that divide us at present, and our goal must be the establishment of Africa's dignity, progress and prosperity.

Proof is therefore positive that the continental union of Africa is an inescapable desideratum if we are determined to move forward to a realization of our hopes and plans for creating a modern society which will give our peoples the opportunity to enjoy a full and satisfying life. The forces that unite us are intrinsic and greater than the superimposed influences that keep us apart. These are the forces that we must enlist and cement for the sake of the trusting millions who look to us, their leaders, to take them out of the poverty, ignorance and disorder left by colonialism into an ordered unity in which freedom and amity can flourish amidst plenty.

Here is a challenge which destiny has thrown out to the leaders of Africa. It is for us to grasp what is a golden opportunity to prove that the genius of the African people can surmount the separatist tendencies in sovereign nationhood by coming together speedily, for the sake of Africa's greater glory and infinite well-being, into a Union of African States.

QUESTIONS

1. What lessons does Nkrumah suggest can be learned from the European experience?
2. What factors lead Nkrumah to believe that no "single state in Africa today can protect its sovereignty against an imperialist aggressor"?
3. To what extent and in what ways does Nkrumah's plan for a United Africa mirror the United States? In what ways is it different?
4. How does Nkrumah's experience of traveling outside of Africa seem to have an impact on his understanding of African identity?

from CONGO MY COUNTRY

Patrice Lumumba

Patrice Lumumba was born in the Belgian Congo in 1925. After attending missionary schools, he worked as a clerk and journalist in Léopoldville and Stanleyville (now Kinshasa and Kisangani). In 1955 he became the head of a regional trade union and joined the Belgian Liberal Party. Lumumba subsequently helped to found the Mouvement National Congolais (MNC). When Belgium announced its plans to grant the Congo independence and instituted local elections, the MNC won a convincing majority. Upon Congolese independence in 1960, Lumumba became the country's first prime minister. His administration was marked by political disruption and turbulence. Within a year, Joseph Mobutu led a military coup (apparently backed by the United States, which believed Lumumba to be a communist) to overthrow Lumumba, who was arrested and died in custody after brutal treatment by his captors.

Congo My Country is a collection of Lumumba's writings and speeches outlining his ideas and plans for the process of decolonizing the Congo's institutions and civil society. It was published in French immediately following Lumumba's arrest, and in English one year later. The writings reflect not only Lumumba's background as a trade unionist but also his engagement with Belgian liberalism.

ECONOMIC INTEGRATION

Equality in the labour market is the dream of all the Congolese; it is a legitimate dream which is in accordance with Article 23 of the *Declaration of Human Rights*: "Everyone, without any discrimination, has the right to equal pay for equal work. Everyone who works has the right to just and favourable remuneration, ensuring for himself and his family an existence worthy of human dignity, supplemented if necessary by other means of social protection."

In general, the Congolese worker has not yet reached his due standard of living. As Governor General Ryckmans has stated recently in an article published in the Colonial press, it is admitted that the wages paid to the natives are still inadequate. At the present time, the majority earn less than 500 francs a month;[1] this can be confirmed from the tariffs of legal minimum wages in various areas; only in Leopoldville can workers earn anything approaching a thousand francs.

The same unsatisfactory state of affairs is found in the various trades, both in the public and private sector. There is ample evidence of this in the recent fiercely-supported wage claims.

My little investigation on this subject has led me to the conclusion that the minimum necessary to sustain life—the absolute minimum for an unskilled worker without a family—is 1,300 francs for food alone, made up as follows: 3 francs for breakfast (one cup of coffee with a few native fritters), twenty francs for the mid-day meal and twenty francs for the evening meal, making a total of forty-three francs per day. This is, of course, on a diet only of manioc leaves or spinach, as a kilogramme of meat of the lowest quality, (generally called servants' meat), costs not less than forty francs.

For a salaried worker of medium social status—the status to which any educated Congolese is entitled—the average monthly household expenditure will vary between 3,000 and 5,000 francs, depending on the size of his family.

Let us see exactly what will be the expenditure, without any luxury, of a middle-grade, *evolué* salaried worker, the father of two children—a household of four; his way of life is no longer primitive and his native diet has been substantially improved by the addition of some items of

144

European diet: coffee, tea, milk, bread, sweet-stuffs, potatoes, vegetables, fruit, meat, etc.:

Breakfast	5 francs per day for four persons =	20 francs
Lunch	30 francs per day for four persons =	120 francs
Dinner	20 francs per day for four persons =	80 francs
		220 francs

Monthly expenditure 220 × 30 days = 6,600 francs

To the cost of food, we must add the other requirements of a family and the education of the children.

The under-nourishment of the Congolese is due solely to the inadequacy of their diet. How is it possible to obtain a varied diet, rich in vitamins, without the necessary financial resources?

The physical and mental health of the people demand an increase in wages.

It should also be noticed, to take an example, that some Congolese *evolués* whose children go to schools belonging to the European system, have to feed and keep their children at virtually the same standard as the children of Europeans of modest means—particularly in regard to clothing. This is in order to avoid harming the children psychologically in their contacts with their European fellow pupils by an excessive difference both in clothing and diet.

These children cannot go to school in rags, barefoot, with pieces of *chikwang*[2] in their hands, since all the children are required to maintain a very high standard of cleanliness, both in regard to their clothing and their persons; they cannot breakfast on *Chikwang* in the classroom while their European comrades are eating bread and jam; besides the teachers would never allow it.

There is a real duel between employers and workers over wages. Employers claim that the Blacks are already earning enough, that their output is inadequate, and that, in these conditions, any increase in wages is unjustified. What is to be done in the face of this clash of interests? In my view, a compromise is essential. The employers undoubtedly have the right to require from their workers a higher output to match the wage which they are claiming. The workers also have the right to demand a fair

145

wage from their employers. If no agreement can be reached between employers and workers, logic requires concessions from both sides.

If the output of Congolese workers is really inadequate, how is it possible to explain the Congo's great economic development? Those vast and prosperous plantations scattered over the country, the roads, bridges, large blocks of flats and other buildings, the operations of the big mining companies, the management of local tax and post offices, etc., all these are surely the product of African labour.

The Europeans bring to the Congo their capital, their intelligence and their experience, whilst the natives supply their energy, muscle and labour power; the European supervises and directs, while the African works hard, loyally and willingly. It is thanks to this steady work and loyal co-operation on the part of the Congolese that these colonial projects are making such progress.

We agree that some workers disregard their contractual obligations and do not improve their output; but we must avoid the sweeping generalisation that the output of the Africans is poor.

Under this heading of productivity, there are two closely-linked conditions which must be fulfilled in order to obtain a better output from all manual or salaried workers:

1. *A good vocational training,* without which it is difficult for an employee to acquire a conscientious attitude to his work. It has been proved that Congolese who have received a suitable vocational or technical training—such as medical and agricultural assistants, trained postal-workers from the postal school, trained male nurses, radio operators from the tele-communications school, and skilled workers from the higher and intermediate vocational schools—are on the whole above the average in efficiency, and most conscientious workers.

Their greater efficiency is due, not only to practice, but also to the fact that they know the technical details of their trade and can solve certain questions on their own without the help of their employer—questions which a mere routine worker would often be unable to solve without that help.

In the interests both of the employers and the workers of the Congo, it is essential to establish the maximum number of vocational and technical schools for trade apprentices so that, in the near or distant future, every worker may become a specialist in his trade. That would provide firms with a body of first-class workers.

A man should not be a jack-of-all-trades as is the case at present in the Congo, where Africans move from one type of employment to another, so that a man who yesterday was a labourer may today become a checker, clerk, male nurse, cashier, stoker, or what have you.

2. *An adequate and fair wage,* a real incentive without which it is illusory to hope for a better output from the workers.

Some manual and salaried workers have said to me: "What is the point of working hard, toiling away uselessly, when our efforts will not be rewarded by an appropriate wage."

I explained to them that, if the manual and salaried workers, as a whole, improved their efficiency, that would increase the profits of the firms and, in consequence, would lead to a raising of wages; for it should not be forgotten that employers are afraid that an increase of wages without a compensating increase in productivity might ruin them. But they made short shrift of this argument: "If your thesis is valid and practicable, how is it that the few top-grade manual and salaried workers who have now reached a standard of efficiency equal to that of European workers are not paid on the same basis as the latter, and do not even receive half the lowest wage paid to Europeans? As those workers are not paid correspondingly, although at present they are only a minority and would not place a heavy burden on the employers, we think it would be Utopian to dream of a general regrading of Congolese wages, even if the Congolese were to double their efficiency."

I would urge those who may try to do slipshod work, on the pretext that they are less well-paid, not to lose heart in this struggle for a better life: that sort of conduct merely weakens our position. The more we increase our efficiency and observe our contractual obligations, the stronger will be our claim. Discouragement does not help the development of a nation. Whatever may be the difficulties which confront us, and they are difficulties with which every nation is familiar, we must continue our efforts with an unshakeable will and with absolute confidence in ourselves.

We shall never be able to improve our situation by laziness, but only by an unyielding and ever-increasing common effort. The men of good will—and there are many of them—must give the lead to the others.

As it is admitted that present wages are inadequate, the most elementary justice demands that this collective claim for higher wages should be granted as far as possible.

The Congolese ask for nothing better than to earn 100 francs a month, provided that, with those 100 francs, they can live more or less decently, meet their children's requirements adequately and have something left over to put aside for the future.

How can a man improve his standard of living, secure decent conditions for his family, pay for his children's education and, in general, enter the ranks of the civilised, with such an inadequate income?

How many really deserving Congolese, to whom the card of civic merit[3] has been granted because their way of life was virtually the same as . . . [illegible] . . . it must be realised that, owing to their straitened circumstances, they are living in huts or rented houses, without the bare minimum of comforts and with their children inadequately provided for, etc. . . .

And how bitter is their disappointment when they find that other people, wealthier but less civilised than themselves, are easily able to obtain those cards which are so much desired by the elite, cards which grant their holders equal status with the Europeans in certain matters?

Is it realised that the main cause of dishonesty among many Congolese (cashier-foremen, tax collectors and officials handling public funds) is their low rate of pay, on which they cannot possibly make ends meet, even with the best will in the world? In these circumstances, even the most honest will not always maintain their standards. Overwhelmed by the problems of living and by hunger, they are less able to resist temptation and they often end by succumbing. Some cashier-foremen are paid from [words illegible] to [illegible] per month and, to crown it all, they are only paid several months in arrears.

It would not be correct to deduce from this that an increase in salaries will automatically eliminate all dishonest practices, and that no African will ever be able to steal or embezzle money, but it has to be admitted, in all objectivity, that the number will be considerably reduced, since the main cause for these malpractices will thus be eliminated.

In the interests of security itself, consideration should be given to the possibility of removing all the factors which may encourage or give rise to crimes of any kind.

It is admitted that some Congolese do earn a good living, but they are only a minority whom I shall ignore since I am concerned with the majority and not with special cases.

It should also be pointed out that the Congo is not the only country in Africa in which the Blacks are less well-paid than the Whites. On the contrary, we are amongst the best administered and happiest colonies in the African continent. Our standard of life is far superior to that of the Africans in some other countries. But that ought not to prevent us from moving forward all the time, since the ambition of Overseas Belgium is to be amongst the leaders in the march towards progress and a humane life.

The Congolese élite have no wish to ignore what has been accomplished; they only wish to be "Belgians" and to be entitled to the same well-being and the same rights, given equal merits, of course. This desire is praiseworthy and in accordance with human justice.

I should also like to reply to the argument which is often put forward by some people according to which (a) Congolese workers already earn much more than workers in metropolitan Belgium and (b) Congolese wages should be based on the Belgian scale.

In regard to the first point, this is true only for a tiny minority. Let us examine the position more closely. In Belgium, the monthly wage of a young clerk with a lower secondary education (i.e. who has not studied classics[4]) varies between 50,000 and 77,000 francs or more, plus cost of living allowance, plus an increment of 1,800 francs every two years, plus promotion every two years if he has a good report. The monthly wage of a servant boy or night watchman varies between 44,200 and 55,400 francs, plus an increment of 800 francs every two years, plus family allowances, plus all other benefits.

In the Congo, the basic wage of a native clerk who has had the same full lower secondary education (four years of secondary school under the Congolese system) as his Belgian colleague, is fixed at 15,000 francs plus thirty per cent cost of living index, plus family allowance, plus promotion every three years, plus annual increment of two, three or three-and-a-half per cent depending on whether his report is good, very good or excellent.

I agree that the general standard of education of a Belgian is superior to that of a native who has had the same schooling in the Congo; that is a question of curriculum.

This comparison between the wage of a Belgian clerk and a Congolese clerk, both of whom have had the same schooling, is sufficient in itself to rebut the assertions of certain people who oppose an increase in African salaries under cover of specious arguments.

As regards the second point, I do not think that it would be quite fair to apply the Belgian salary scale in the Congo, for the simple reason that the cost of living in Africa is higher than in Belgium (with the exception, of course, of the mass of the people who live on a lower diet), and because the Blacks pay more than the Europeans for many articles imported from Europe. That may appear strange at first sight, but it is a fact. Whereas Europeans are often granted discounts in the shops (e.g. for large families) these are never granted to the Africans, who always buy at full price and are frequently cheated by unscrupulous foreign traders who profit by the ignorance of the Africans by putting their prices up during the first three days after each pay day.

In short, wages in the Congo should be based not on the Belgian scale but on local requirements. It is impossible to compare two sets of circumstances which are fundamentally different.

To sum up:

1. The wages of all African workers should be increased to keep pace with the cost of living, in view of the fact that this is increasing much faster than wage rates;
2. The democratic formula "equal pay for equal work" should be applied, in order to get rid of any idea of racial discrimination.

ENDNOTES

1. 140 francs to £1.
2. *Chikwang:* A cheap cereal food that forms part of the subsistence diet of the poorest people.
3. The Civic Merit Card.
4. Lumumba is referring to academic subjects.

QUESTIONS

1. What kind of diet does Lumumba say can be obtained for 1,300 francs per month?
2. What, according to Lumumba, is the difference in salary between a clerk in Belgium and a "native clerk" in the Congo?

3. How is change in the educational system related to the decolonization of the economy, according to Lumumba?

4. Why might some people in the United States have thought Lumumba was a communist? Do you see any evidence for that view in this selection?

152

OAU CHARTER

The Organization for African Unity

The Organization for African Unity was founded in 1963 with thirty-two states as members. It expanded earlier African alliances, including two opposing blocs known as the Monrovia Group and the Casablanca Group. Although various states held differing views on the feasibility of putting into practice African political unification, they met in Addis Ababa, Ethiopia to construct a framework for cooperation. The Organization for African Unity lasted until 1999, when it was replaced by the Africa Union, an organization with increased interventionary and peace-keeping powers.

The OAU Charter reflects the structure of post-World War II diplomacy and the importance of framing post-colonial politics within the United Nations context. It outlines the administrative procedures by which the organization will run, as well as the principles by which its actions will be guided. Faced with the challenge of balancing divergent views, the charter seeks above all to offer a forum for discussion among member states.

We, the Heads of African States and Governments assembled in the City of Addis Ababa, Ethiopia,

Convinced that it is the inalienable right of all people to control their own destiny,

---

Adopted May 25, 1963 in the city of Addis Abdaba, Ethiopia.

Conscious of the fact that freedom, equality, justice and dignity are essential objectives for the achievement of the legitimate aspirations of the African peoples,

Conscious of our responsibility to harness the natural and human resources of our continent for the total advancement of our peoples in all spheres of human endeavour,

Inspired by a common determination to promote understanding among our peoples and cooperation among our states in response to the aspirations of our peoples for brother-hood and solidarity, in a larger unity transcending ethnic and national differences,

Convinced that, in order to translate this determination into a dynamic force in the cause of human progress, conditions for peace and security must be established and maintained,

Determined to safeguard and consolidate the hard-won independence as well as the sovereignty and territorial integrity of our states, and to fight against neo-colonialism in all its forms,

Dedicated to the general progress of Africa,

Persuaded that the Charter of the United Nations and the Universal Declaration of Human Rights, to the Principles of which we reaffirm our adherence, provide a solid foundation for peaceful and positive cooperation among States,

Desirous that all African States should henceforth unite so that the welfare and well-being of their peoples can be assured,

Resolved to reinforce the links between our states by establishing and strengthening common institutions,

Have agreed to the present Charter.

ESTABLISHMENT

Article I

1. The High Contracting Parties do by the present Charter establish an Organization to be known as the ORGANIZATION OF AFRICAN UNITY.

2. The Organization shall include the Continental African States, Madagascar and other Islands surrounding Africa.

PURPOSES

Article II

1. The Organization shall have the following purposes:
   (a) To promote the unity and solidarity of the African States;
   (b) To coordinate and intensify their cooperation and efforts to achieve a better life for the peoples of Africa;
   (c) To defend their sovereignty, their territorial integrity and independence;
   (d) To eradicate all forms of colonialism from Africa; and
   (e) To promote international cooperation, having due regard to the Charter of the United Nations and the Universal Declaration of Human Rights.
2. To these ends, the Member States shall coordinate and harmonize their general policies, especially in the following fields:
   (a) Political and diplomatic cooperation;
   (b) Economic cooperation, including transport and communications;
   (c) Educational and cultural cooperation;
   (d) Health, sanitation and nutritional cooperation;
   (e) Scientific and technical cooperation; and
   (f) Cooperation for defence and security.

PRINCIPLES

Article III

The Member States, in pursuit of the purposes stated in Article II solemnly affirm and declare their adherence to the following principles:

1. The sovereign equality of all Member States.
2. Non-interference in the internal affairs of States.
3. Respect for the sovereignty and territorial integrity of each State and for its inalienable right to independent existence.

4. Peaceful settlement of disputes by negotiation, mediation, conciliation or arbitration.
5. Unreserved condemnation, in all its forms, of political assassination as well as of subversive activities on the part of neighbouring States or any other States.
6. Absolute dedication to the total emancipation of the African territories which are still dependent.
7. Affirmation of a policy of non-alignment with regard to all blocs.

MEMBERSHIP

Article IV

Each independent sovereign African State shall be entitled to become a Member of the Organization.

RIGHTS AND DUTIES OF MEMBER STATES

Article V

All Member States shall enjoy equal rights and have equal duties.

Article VI

The Member States pledge themselves to observe scrupulously the principles enumerated in Article III of the present Charter.

INSTITUTIONS

Article VII

The Organization shall accomplish its purposes through the following principal institutions:

1. The Assembly of Heads of State and Government.
2. The Council of Ministers.
3. The General Secretariat.

4. The Commission of Mediation, Conciliation and Arbitration.

THE ASSEMBLY OF HEADS OF STATE AND GOVERNMENT

Article VIII

The Assembly of Heads of State and Government shall be the supreme organ of the Organization. It shall, subject to the provisions of this Charter, discuss matters of common concern to Africa with a view to coordinating and harmonizing the general policy of the Organization. It may in addition review the structure, functions and acts of all the organs and any specialized agencies which may be created in accordance with the present Charter.

Article IX

The Assembly shall be composed of the Heads of State and Government or their duly accredited representatives and it shall meet at least once a year. At the request of any Member State and on approval by a two-thirds majority of the Member States, the Assembly shall meet in extraordinary session.

Article X

1. Each Member State shall have one vote.
2. All resolutions shall be determined by a two-thirds majority of the Members of the Organization.
3. Questions of procedure shall require a simple majority. Whether or not a question is one of procedure shall be determined by a simple majority of all Member States of the Organization.
4. Two-thirds of the total membership of the Organization shall form a quorum at any meeting of the Assembly.

Article XI

The Assembly shall have the power to determine its own rules of procedure.

THE COUNCIL OF MINISTERS

Article XII

1. The Council of Ministers shall consist of Foreign Ministers or other Ministers as are designated by the Governments of Member States.
2. The Council of Ministers shall meet at least twice a year. When requested by any Member State and approved by two-thirds of all Member States, it shall meet in extraordinary session.

Article XIII

1. The Council of Ministers shall be responsible to the Assembly of Heads of State and Government. It shall be entrusted with the responsibility of preparing conferences of the Assembly.
2. It shall take cognisance of any matter referred to it by the Assembly. It shall be entrusted with the implementation of the decision of the Assembly of Heads of State and Government. It shall coordinate inter-African cooperation in accordance with the instructions of the Assembly conformity with Article II (2) of the present Charter.

Article XIV

1. Each Member State shall have one vote.
2. All resolutions shall be determined by a simple majority of the members of the Council of Ministers.
3. Two-thirds of the total membership of the Council of Ministers shall form a quorum for any meeting of the Council.

Article XV

The Council shall have the power to determine its own rules of procedure.

GENERAL SECRETARIAT

Article XVI

There shall be a Secretary-General of the Organization, who shall be appointed by the Assembly of Heads of State and Government. The Secretary-General shall direct the affairs of the Secretariat.

Article XVII

There shall be one or more Assistant Secretaries-General of the Organization, who shall be appointed by the Assembly of Heads of State and Government.

Article XVIII

The functions and conditions of service of the Secretary-General, of the Assistant Secretaries-General and other employees of the Secretariat shall be governed by the provisions of this Charter and the regulations approved by the Assembly of Heads of State and Government.

1. In the performance of their duties the Secretary-General and the staff shall not seek or receive instructions from any government or from any other authority external to the Organization. They shall refrain from any action which might reflect on their position as international officials responsible only to the Organization.
2. Each member of the Organization undertakes to respect the exclusive character of the responsibilities of the Secretary-General and the staff and not to seek to influence them in the discharge of their responsibilities.

COMMISSION OF MEDIATION, CONCILIATION AND ARBITRATION

Article XIX

Member States pledge to settle all disputes among themselves by peaceful means and, to this end decide to establish a Commission of Mediation,

Conciliation and Arbitration, the composition of which and conditions of service shall be defined by a separate Protocol to be approved by the Assembly of Heads of State and Government. Said Protocol shall be regarded as forming an integral part of the present Charter. . . .

SIGNATURE AND RATIFICATION OF CHARTER

Article XXIV

1. This Charter shall be open for signature to all independent sovereign African States and shall be ratified by the signatory States in accordance with their respective constitutional processes.
2. The original instrument, done, if possible in African languages, in English and French, all texts being equally authentic, shall be deposited with the Government of Ethiopia which shall transmit certified copies thereof to all independent sovereign African States.
3. Instruments of ratification shall be deposited with the Government of Ethiopia, which shall notify all signatories of each such deposit.

ENTRY INTO FORCE

Article XXV

This Charter shall enter into force immediately upon receipt by the Government of Ethiopia of the instruments of ratification from two-thirds of the signatory States.

REGISTRATION OF CHARTER

Article XXVI

This Charter shall, after due ratification, be registered with the Secretariat of the United Nations through the Government of Ethiopia in conformity with Article 102 of the Charter of the United Nations.

INTERPRETATION OF THE CHARTER

Article XXVII

Any question which may arise concerning the interpretation of this Charter shall be decided by a vote of two-thirds of the Assembly of Heads of State and Government of the Organization.

ADHESION AND ACCESSION

Article XXVIII

1. Any independent sovereign African State may at any time notify the Secretary-General of its intention to adhere or accede to this Charter.
2. The Secretary-General shall, on receipt of such notification, communicate a copy of it to all the Member States. Admission shall be decided by a simple majority of the Member States. The decision of each Member State shall be transmitted to the Secretary-General, who shall, upon receipt of the required number of votes, communicate the decision to the State concerned.

MISCELLANEOUS

Article XXIX

The working languages of the Organization and all its institutions shall be, if possible African languages, English and French, Arabic and Portuguese.

Article XXX

The Secretary-General may accept, on behalf of the Organization, gifts, bequests and other donations made to the Organization, provided that this is approved by the Council of Ministers.

Article XXXI

The Council of Ministers shall decide on the privileges and immunities to be accorded to the personnel of the Secretariat in the respective territories of the Member States.

CESSATION OF MEMBERSHIP

Article XXXI

Any State which desires to renounce its membership shall forward a written notification to the Secretary-General. At the end of one year from the date of such notification, if not withdrawn, the Charter shall cease to apply with respect to the renouncing State, which shall thereby cease to belong to the Organization.

AMENDMENT OF THE CHARTER

Article XXXII

This Charter may be amended or revised if any Member State makes a written request to the Secretary-General to that effect; provided, however, that the proposed amendment is not submitted to the Assembly for consideration until all the Member States have been duly notified of it and a period of one year has elapsed. Such an amendment shall not be effective unless approved by at least two-thirds of all the Member States.

IN FAITH WHEREOF, We, the Heads of African States and Governments have signed this Charter.

Done in the City of Addis Ababa, Ethiopia,
25ᵗʰ day of May, 1963

QUESTIONS

1. What is the OAU's policy toward African territories that are not independent as of 1963?
2. Who is permitted to join the OAU and how can they do so?
3. In what ways does the OAU charter reference Africa's colonial experience and the transition to post-colonial government?
4. What challenges might be encountered in implementing the structures oulined by the charter?